PRAISE FOR
PAUL HILTZ, AMANDA LUCEY, AND *UPHEAVAL*

"A great American business story of overcoming adversity that shows how a community can come together and win. It's amazing what people can do if nobody wants the credit."

—BILL BARKER
former president and publisher of Naples Daily News

"Paul Hiltz is an incredible leader and person. His work with NCH has been transformative. The pages in this book provide insights that every leader should follow and focus on. Paul and his team led NCH through crisis times, while rebranding and strengthening the healthcare organization; improving quality and creating strategic partnerships for the future."

—SCOTT BECKER
Founder, Becker's Healthcare

"Paul is a visionary CEO, and this book is a testament to his vision. *Upheaval* showcases an authentic and empowering leadership style that puts patients and communities first. Hiltz is known for creating high levels of medical staff satisfaction, loyalty, and engagement. In fact, one of Hiltz's signature strategies was providing significant support for primary care physicians during the COVID-19 pandemic, a strategy that has paid dividends to NCH. Overall, *Upheaval* shows how developing community trust is essential to providing effective healthcare, especially in tumultuous times."

—MICHAEL CONNELLY

CEO Emeritus Mercy Health

"*Upheaval* captivates readers like a gripping story in a Tom Clancy novel. It is indeed a must-read for anybody in the healthcare industry. Anyone aspiring to make an impact in a leadership role should take the time to delve into this marvelous work."

—DR. SURENDER R. NERAVETLA

Heart Surgeon; Author, Salt Kills

"Amanda is highly strategic, a creative thinker, and a master problem solver. If there's a mountain to climb, she's the certified guide you want by your side."

—CHRISTA PITTS

CEO and co-Founder of The Lumistella Company, home of The Elf on the Shelf, Elf Pets, and Elf Mates brands

PAUL HILTZ FACHE
AMANDA R. LUCEY

UPHEAVAL

CRAFTING
A CULTURE
& MANAGING
YOUR MESSAGE
THROUGH A CRISIS

Forbes | Books

Published by Forbes Books, Charleston, South Carolina.
An imprint of Advantage Media Group.

Forbes Books is a registered trademark, and the Forbes Books colophon is a trademark of Forbes Media, LLC.

Printed in the United States of America.

10 9 8 7 6 5 4 3 2 1

ISBN: 978-1-64225-786-1 (Hardcover)
ISBN: 978-1-64225-785-4 (eBook)

Library of Congress Control Number: 2024920747

Cover design by Lance Buckley.
Layout design by Matthew Morse.

This custom publication is intended to provide accurate information and the opinions of the author in regard to the subject matter covered. It is sold with the understanding that the publisher, Forbes Books, is not engaged in rendering legal, financial, or professional services of any kind. If legal advice or other expert assistance is required, the reader is advised to seek the services of a competent professional.

Since 1917, Forbes has remained steadfast in its mission to serve as the defining voice of entrepreneurial capitalism. Forbes Books, launched in 2016 through a partnership with Advantage Media, furthers that aim by helping business and thought leaders bring their stories, passion, and knowledge to the forefront in custom books. Opinions expressed by Forbes Books authors are their own. To be considered for publication, please visit **books.Forbes.com**.

On March 11, 2021, Rev. Jennie Thomas, director of spiritual care services at NCH, rang a bell 157 times to remember each patient we lost to COVID-19 during the crisis unfolding in the pages ahead.

It was a solemn moment like the bell-ringing tradition at the World Trade Center. Both were tragic events. Both events were unimaginably brutal. Both unexpected. Both birthed heroes who ran toward the danger.

During the pandemic, two thousand frontline healthcare workers slugged it out for over two years with this invisible, malevolent evil, including 1,350 nurses involved in direct patient care. Our total workforce consists of about 4,900 heroes.

This solemn recognition honored the lives lost. Yet the event did more. It was a fitting tribute to the sacrifices that every frontline worker and loyal staff member made. We would fight any community threat with this care team.

They represent the spirit of goodness itself, in every way.

ACKNOWLEDGEMENTS

From Paul and Amanda

A special thank you to the NCH Board of Trustees, to everyone who participated in interviews for the book, to our SWFL community, to the NCH team, all friends of NCH, and to all healthcare heroes. We are in awe of you and everything you accomplished during COVID. Thank you to everyone who helped make this book possible.

From Paul

A special thank you to my first mentor who helped launch my healthcare career, Dan Rissing. Thank you to all my family, friends, and colleagues—I'm grateful for their unconditional support.

From Amanda

Thank you to my family, especially Vincent and Charlotte, friends, mentors, coaches, colleagues, and my team. I'm so thankful to have the love and support from so many who have helped me on this journey. We don't create alone, and I am grateful to be surrounded by talented teams that inspire me daily.

CONTENTS

PART 1
EMERGING PROBLEMS

APPENDIX
COMMUNICATIONS PLANNING

FOREWORD

BY SCOTT LUTGERT

Community leader Scott Lutgert

I have had the honor of leading the board of trustees of Naples Comprehensive Health (NCH) for the past several years, following the enlightened leadership of Mariann MacDonald.

The first crisis Paul and Amanda describe in *Upheaval* was an intense debate about the use of hospitalist physicians in our

1

hospitals, which ripped the bonds of trust between citizens, doctors, and our hospitals.

Our administrative team had done a nice job for NCH for over twenty years; both administrators were well respected in the industry and Naples. For whatever reason, they locked down policies that the doctors and community didn't like, which went from disagreement to outrage like a forest fire.

The administrators felt strongly that the community's primary physicians should agree to enable the hospitalist doctors to fully care for their inpatients. This is another great learning moment for hospitals and communities nationwide. When you read this story, you will see how a group of upset physicians can marshal an entire community to respond to something they perceive as heavy handed and dictatorial. Dozens of concierge primary care doctors called for the public's support. Other doctors and their patients rallied to support them.

Simmering in the background was the administration's decision to walk away from the Neighborhood Health Clinic, another decision I still need to understand. That upset a lot of people.

Upheaval does an excellent job of acknowledging and saluting the heroes of the management crisis and the heroes within the horrors of the coming pandemic. We learned that our clinical teams not only have a great capacity for grace under pressure but are also willing to openly confront continuous danger.

But Jay Baker and I want to be sure that folks who read this book understand how intense the community anger had become. This community was ready to tar and feather the board, the administration, and anyone else who fell asleep at the wheel of leading their community hospital.

This had become an unbelievably aggressive reaction from the community.

The main flashpoint criticisms pointed at the following:

- The creation of a hostile environment for the physicians.
- Abandoning support of the Neighborhood Clinic without discussion.
- Not allowing concierge doctors to see their patients in the hospital.
- But there was more. This had become, as I described, a forest fire.
- Protests were being organized in neighborhood meetings throughout the region.
- Yard signs attacking the hospitals were going up.
- The news media lost faith and trust in the leadership and were asking who owned the hospitals anyway.
- Doctors were leaving the hospital, dropping privileges, some never to return.
- Loyal donors stopped their support.
- Hospital finances were at crisis level.
- Doctors were encouraging their patients to protest the hospital policies.
- Protests in the park were being promoted and aired live on local television news.
- Critical letters to the editor were published regularly.
- Morale had been all but destroyed throughout NCH.
- Past hospital leaders were airing their criticism.
- City and county leaders were calling for the hospital leadership to explain itself.

Jay Baker and I (and many others) warned them, saying, "If you keep doing this, you'll lose your jobs …"

Yet, the administration continued to claim that these policies would *make it better* and *have patience. Everything will work out; the outrage will go away.* Well, that never happened. And the board finally said, "Look, we have a responsibility here to the entire community, and these procedures aren't working out. If you don't want to change them, you got to go."

While that does not diminish what this team previously accomplished, they stubbornly held on to their decision. As protests throughout the community and continuous news coverage reached a crescendo, the board lost faith and fired the top two executives.

Then, board chair Mariann MacDonald asked Jay Baker and me, who had been vocal critics of the hospital, to come in and lead the organization. We would reshape the board and bring in new leadership there as well.

I asked my friend and colleague Jay Baker to comment on the upheaval. Jay and I had both served on the NCH board years back. When the management upheaval occurred, Mariann MacDonald beckoned us back onto the board to help solve the community crisis.

"There were a lot of heroic acts when everything went south with the management. Then later, navigating the horrors of a lethal, unknown, unseen monster, courageous heroes were everywhere."

Jay Baker is a calm, businesslike, sensible man. But he, too, was angry. We are both people of reason. The Baker name is on both NCH hospitals: the NCH Baker Downtown Hospital and the Jay & Patty Baker Patient Care Tower in the NCH North Naples Hospital. They have been the most generous and steadfast donors in this community's history.

I've never seen an angrier community anywhere in the country than Naples during these years, where everything went wrong. I've lived in New York, I've lived in Milwaukee, I've lived in St. Louis and been exposed to some of the top leaders in US healthcare, and I've never seen anything quite like this.

It seemed as if these people lost track of who and where they were and who they worked for. You're not the only hospital, you're not the only choice, you're not the only one. So yeah, you need the people's trust to exist.

That trust was already gone, smothered in the jeers and boos of protests in the city park. Smothered in the cursing phone calls I received from my community friends. Smothered in the doctors coming to my home, half in tears, half in rage. Smothered in the quiet placement of yard signs attacking NCH in hundreds of neighborhoods.

These two events back-to-back were unprecedented. So it was a very rough situation. But Scott and I, as a team, redid the board and made many beautiful things happen. Scott is a terrific chairman, and they were compelled to put the two of us on. We were the most vocal of the legions of angry citizens.

I'm sure they didn't love the two of us going on the board, but they had no choice. And then we redid the leadership and the board. Scott brought in three new members. I brought in three new members, and we kept some terrific people still on the board, reshaping the governing body. The community would never accept that old board anymore. Everyone involved was late to the party.

Many colleagues whispered that everything should be redone. Everything. Well, everything didn't have to be redone.

Sometimes, you are thrust into a situation where you must make tough decisions. We were very fortunate that it worked out, but we trusted the rest of the board, Paul, and his team. We gave them the tools to get it done.

You have to remember and keep doing all the good things. You keep that trust because we've seen what can happen when you lose faith.

Our hospitals are much better today than ever, and the future is much brighter. So, enduring terrible problems and then facing COVID-19 right after it, we emerged weary, intact, and changed.

Paul and Amanda have compiled this compelling story so we will always remember it, never again lose sight of who owns the hospitals, and never again risk community trust.

—Jay Baker

Jay and Patty Baker

Mariann also retained Amanda Lucey, who did crisis communications just in time to help pick up the pieces and communicate the scope of the national search. Mariann, board members Jay Baker, Kevin Beebe, and Michael Wynn, along with several great doctors and community leaders, joined me in the monthslong executive search.

Months later, we found Paul Hiltz. I thought he was the perfect fit because he could go out and talk to people.

Reflecting on it, I had only one little problem with Paul. I told the recruiters, "I don't see any red flags. I mean, the guy looks perfect. I must dive down more, but he listens. He's calm, smart, and a leader. He could bring culture into the hospitals and bring morale back. I think the guy is very, very good."

So, Paul initially did an intense listening tour, precisely what he should have done.

He had to change that whole culture, get everybody on the same team, and work together toward quality healthcare and patient satisfaction, the benchmark of the board's decisions. If the procedure or initiative would improve quality and patient satisfaction, then it made sense. If it didn't, we probably didn't want to do it. And the whole board was united on that philosophy and mission, and so was Paul. So it was easy when everybody had the same goals.

Paul and his team went to every civic club and community organization they could. They made a presentation, and people instantly saw that this leader cared, was open, and would listen. So, he brought a lot of people around quickly. Now, some of the doctors took a bit longer, but ultimately, he was able to do it. He also made some changes in his administrative team. He was out in the community. I mean, he's tireless.

Every spare minute, Paul would be on the floors, all shifts, talking to everybody in the hospital and letting people know he would listen. He wasn't just a dictator. He wanted to know their problems, how things were going, what could be improved, etc. They started to understand after a while. It was going to be implemented and happened.

Then, just as we were getting back some of the trust we had lost, the nightmare began. I can tell you that every board member knew we were in trouble. We weathered a problematic management transition, which was severe, but the pandemic was a level of horror no one expected.

Clinically, we knew we had the best team in the country working on it. And board members are business leaders, so we understood how cataclysmic this could be from many different viewpoints. Financially, it was the biggest challenge in the organization's history. Luckily, the recovery of trust following the management upheaval had begun just when that support became essential. Paul continued his speaking tour, but the subject of his message changed. Everyone in the community was thirsty for information about this disease.

The uncertainty and absolute shock we all felt when this monster came ashore in Naples are still felt today in a newly energized sense of community in Naples and Collier County. The beast was bigger than us.

We have lived through the existential threat. As board members, our job, as always, was to ensure that everything our clinical teams needed was there. Our leadership in the community helped us to convey the message that this was virulent, deadly, and coming fast. My wife, Simone, deeply involved with children's health, women's health, and emergency shelters in her community life, kept her radar up for me, helping me understand community sentiment.

Well, of course, at the beginning of COVID-19, it was extraordinarily terrifying because we didn't know what we were facing, and we didn't know how many people would die. And if you look at what was happening in Europe, Spain, and Italy, that first variant was totally out of control.

Imagine a constant line of desperately ill people arriving by every conveyance possible to the emergency department, desperately struggling, day after day after day after day. And honestly, not having a playbook on how to clinically encounter the threat.

We were extraordinarily vigilant, scrambling to get a lot of ventilators, watching the nightmare unfold in New York. Fortunately, later, we learned we didn't need the ventilators. Still, we had plenty of them, and we were ahead of the curve, paying attention and eliminating the nightmare scenarios of insufficient equipment and supplies. We prepared a M.A.S.H-like hospital tent for overflow.

Now, remember that there was no vaccine at the outset. Extremely infectious, every single person in the hospital was at risk of contracting COVID-19 every day, and their families were as well. We knew the nightmare had begun. We were unsure of our oxygen suppliers' ability to keep us supplied.

Because of infection control, we shifted some air-conditioning systems so that the air from the room didn't go out into the hallway. We got masks for everybody and put in urgent procedures to protect people. We were on this day and night. We tracked our caseload and the patient demographics of patients in the hospital. We stopped elective surgeries because we were slammed every day, busy taking care of very sick people.

Finances became difficult, and revenue was lost. But we said we'd come out of this at some point. Our board locked arms and pledged that *we must take care of the community and do what's right now, and it'll be okay later. We're not sure how, but we'll figure it out.*

A leap of faith.

So, we kept our major projects going. During the COVID-19 threat, many hospitals postponed development projects, but we did not pause. We kept the momentum of quality projects, a new heart hospital, cancer advancements, women's health advancements, and a vital new medical record system. We avoided reducing salaries and layoffs as we shifted personnel to meet the needs. Everybody was locked down. Our reports reflect that among our staff, only two cases of COVID-19 were acquired in the hospital after two years of grappling with this deadly plague. I think that's extraordinary.

I cannot imagine a scarier crisis, and I cannot tell you how proud I am of all the doctors, hospital staff, leadership, and this community for stepping up when we needed it. Our primary care physicians volunteered to come in and help whenever needed. Community leaders, especially restauranteur Paul Fleming, who never let up on his continuous support, donated and delivered thousands of meals to the hospitals. Donors rallied, bringing financial support back to historically high levels. People all over the region called us, asking how they could help.

We must view the world through stories. So, what story should we see the world through?

I am delighted that Paul, Amanda, and Forbes have composed this powerful story. We all see the world through stories. This story can help community leaders across America as we share these priceless lessons in community leadership and community connections because, as Paul and Amanda say, we may see this dark visitor again.

FOREWORD

BY BRYAN MURPHEY, MD

Bryan Murphey, MD

Dr. Murphey graduated from the University College Dublin School of Medicine and Medical Science in 1997, performing his residency at Cleveland Clinic in internal medicine from 1997 to 2000.

He practiced internal medicine in Naples for twenty-four years, serving as ambulatory chief medical officer for NCH and on the board of Community Health Partners, the regional physician contracting group. During the challenging days of the leadership crisis at NCH and the horrors of the pandemic, Dr. Murphey served as the interim chief medical officer and helped lead the medical staff and the entire healthcare organization during its darkest hours.

As we publish this, we are still decompressing. Recalling these events brings back some vivid memories and emotional artifacts that will never be forgotten. They come in 3D waves and can be triggered with just a word or a name.

My hat is off to the entire medical staff for their courageous practice of medicine during the most difficult of circumstances. And to our clinical staff and the many sacrifices made to save lives and heal the entire community, to all our employees, *thank you*.

I must commend the members of our board of directors, past and present, for their gifted leadership during our tortured journey through the management upheaval and then the pandemic. I offer special applause for Mariann MacDonald for her decade of service as board chair. Her careful guidance set the stage for community healing ably assumed by Scott Lutgert.

You will find stories of heroism, courage, resilience, and perseverance, with powerful lessons for managers and community leaders about the importance of community collaboration and communication.

The board chose a healer, Paul Hiltz, when they selected this man to lead the organization. He has led the community back together and brought the healthcare organization to a place where we can fully enjoy the faithful support, confidence, and understanding of the doctors, the management, and the people of Southwest Florida.

This book reads like an adventure because it was an adventure. You will feel our humanity was made vulnerable by COVID-19 and perhaps feel a greater appreciation for the struggle all healthcare teams face—and will one day face again.

We have more work to do to heal the healthcare gap for our communities' vulnerable and marginalized populations, and I sincerely hope you will be moved to help remedy this in your hometown.

BOARD OF TRUSTEES
2023–2024 · NCH SYSTEM

ABOUT THE AUTHORS

PAUL W. HILTZ, MHA, FACHE

If we as a team treat each other like family, and we treat our patients like we would want our family members treated, and if we treat the organization as our home, then we're going to win.

—PAUL HILTZ

From Northern Kentucky, Paul Hiltz attended Xavier University for graduate school in health administration. He's also a Fellow of the American College of Healthcare Executives. Hiltz's career has taken him to roles as the CEO of medical groups, accountable care organizations, and acute care hospitals in highly competitive markets. Paul has been described as one of the best turnaround healthcare executives in America.

Before being selected to lead NCH, he was president and CEO of Mercy Medical Center in Canton, Ohio.

He grew up in Erlanger, Kentucky, a fifteen-minute drive from Cincinnati. His dad, Bob, received the Bronze Star during World War II and later worked in finance for Xavier University. His mom, Anne, was a stay-at-home mom. Hiltz has six siblings. He and his wife of twenty-five years, Kristen, have four children.

Hiltz also maintained prominent positions on multiple professional and community associations, including the board of directors at E. F. Hutton & Co. and the Springfield, Ohio, Chamber of Commerce. In addition to his accolades, he received the 2017 Distinguished Alumni Service Award from the Xavier Graduate Program in Health Administration for outstanding service to the program.

AMANDA LUCEY, CEO, THE PARTNERSHIP

Share your story to encourage others on the journey. Inspire other leaders. After all, supporting each other in business keeps us all going.

—AMANDA LUCEY

Amanda is a change agent. She's been a communications leader, providing strategic public relations, branding and corporate communications for clients and companies across the country for over 20 years.

Amanda is CEO of The Partnership, Atlanta's oldest privately held marketing and brand communications agency, established in 1979.

A progressive thought leader on branding in a new era of organizational communications and an accomplished entrepreneur, she founded Moxie Media and Marketing in 2012 (DBA M3 Effect). The company grew tremendously within its first five years. To accelerate her vision in 2018, Amanda acquired The Partnership. The firm is one of the fastest-growing female-owned agencies in the Southeast and a top-10 advertising agency in Atlanta and Southwest Florida. The agency orchestrates integrated solutions across branding, communications, advertising, public relations, crisis management and digital development. The Partnership also developed a product: Partnership 360™, a proprietary analytics dashboard.

In 2021, The Partnership opened a second location in Naples, Florida. The firm now has representation in Ohio, Pennsylvania, Georgia, and Florida.

Prior to becoming a business owner and CEO Amanda held executive roles with both the U.K. and U.S. governments. She was the Vice Consul, Head of Political, Press and Public Affairs for the British Consulate General, in which she managed all media relations strategies and delivered the UK's policy and public diplomacy priorities. She also served as a media correspondent and director of communications for the U.S. government and has extensive public affairs experience. Prior to working in D.C., Amanda worked for the Georgia General Assembly House of Representatives. Amanda has extensive marketing experience. Her background includes service as the Director of Communications and Public Relations for the Southeast Dairy Association, a marketing organization promoting milk and dairy products. She's also led teams in consulting roles with the Georgia Department of Labor and the DeKalb Economic Development Authority.

Amanda has worked on several political campaigns and served as the marketing chair for various nonprofit organizations. She serves on the National Small Business Association Leadership Council, the University of West Georgia Board of Trustees and is involved in various CEO roundtables and nonprofits.

As a strategic brand communicator, marketer, keynote speaker and media relations professional, Amanda shares stories and empowers others to craft a culture of curiosity that will create the best strategic creative and communications solutions. Her motto: be hungry, keep hustling, and stay humble.

The Partnership has been recognized for excellence by Inc. 5000's Fastest Growing Companies, by AIGA, Addys, the American Advertising Federation, AVA Digital Awards, CLIO Awards, EFFIE Worldwide, New York Festivals, One Show, Radio Mercury, the Art Directors Club of New York, the Sawyer Award and the US Film Festival, Ragan's Crisis Communications Awards, and most recently Amanda has been recognized by PR Daily as a Top Women in Marketing for 2024.

Amid the COVID-19 pandemic, Amanda's expertise in navigating change and crisis communication became invaluable to brands. She's one of the leading crisis communications and media training experts in the nation.

WHEN THE UNEXPECTED HAPPENS

Naples, Florida's Gulf Coast cosmopolitan community, enjoys top rankings of America's highest quality of life. Wonderful soft white powder beaches with daily deposits of colorful shells, sunshine, crystal blue water, and amazing marine life. Everywhere you look are magnificent housing developments, great hotels, world-class restaurants, golf courses, and outstanding schools. It seems like Naples has it all, including top-rated healthcare.

But this *canary in the cage* begins to chirp. In the middle of a top management change, a worldwide pandemic looms. Naples was not the first community to be impacted. We could listen to the canary weeks before the first case showed up in Southwest Florida. New York City was chaos.

A frequent metaphor in our culture, the phrase canary in the cage suggests an early warning, threat, or alert. Decades ago, miners would bring a canary for work deep underground not only because they spread joy and a sense of well-being but also because of their sensitivity to the air. They became pets to the miners, who showed great affection for their companions above and below the earth. *Smithsonian* magazine reported that the anatomy of the canary allows them to get a dose of oxygen when they inhale and another when they exhale. They get a double dose of air and any poisons the air might contain, "so miners would get an earlier warning than with other creatures."[1]

Even in the early days of our work in Naples, we sensed that this situation, the rapid gathering of cooperative strength by the leadership of a highly rated community hospital organization, could present national implications and may well signal a new day not just in healthcare but in business and community leadership generally.

America's healthcare providers may soon face a choice: awaken to a different, more enlightened way of doing business or face another pandemic situation as unprepared as in 2020–2022.

The story that unfolded here took various forms at every one of America's 2,903 community hospitals. Healthcare leaders, as well as healthcare consumers, can see how one very attentive community gathered as never before to deal with this life-and-death situation.

---

1   Kat Eschner, "The Story of the Real Canary in the Coal Mine," *Smithsonian*, December 30, 2016, accessed September 1, 2021, https://www.Smithsonianmag.com/smart-news/story-real-canary-coal-mine-180961570/.

NCH has two acute care hospitals: NCH Downtown Baker Hospital in Naples, Florida,
and NCH North Naples Hospital.

Naples Comprehensive Health is one of the most forward-looking healthcare organizations in the country. More than just a few hospitals, it is an alliance of more than nine hundred independent physicians and medical facilities in dozens of locations throughout Collier County and Southwest Florida. We offer advanced comprehensive care and embrace new, effective ideas in medical care and healing.

And despite the canary chirping in the cage, it happened so quickly that people were stunned.

The management gets the double dose of air and, thankfully, had already begun a new day of openness, community and physician partnership, and an appeal for confidence and understanding. They tested the air around them. Other hospitals, once competitors, became eager partners in the face of this threat. The board of trustees was alert and gathered vital community leaders together.

Naples created a pluralistic, collaborative organization just in time. Led by the physicians, a war room strategy developed among all the community providers, and a new spirit of openness and communication, vital in a pandemic, matured.

We quickly got to work engaging the entire community. A canary comes to mind, and it's not Tweety Bird. There was national dialogue, and at face value, the messages were mixed. This will go away soon to duck and cover. We chose to duck and cover early and began to ramp up the changes we needed to make to fight the pandemic. We needed the community.

Double, double toil and trouble;
Fire burn, and cauldron bubble.[2]

—MACBETH *BY WILLIAM SHAKESPEARE*

The ingredients were all in the cauldron now. Each ingredient had power, but when all were combined over fire, it got serious. Locking down society, wearing masks, creating isolation rooms, and employee morale hitting new lows. At first, there was a shortage of personal protective garments and proper masks. Some left employment to be with their families.

Recruitment became difficult. Nurses worked double shifts. The news media covered every chirp, and finances looked bad. The healthcare world has fragile margins that do not react well to chaos.

---

2   Poetry Foundation, "Song of the Witches: "Double, Double Toil and Trouble,"
     accessed March 11, 2024, https://www.poetryfoundation.org/poems/43189/
     song-of-the-witches-double-double-toil-and-trouble.

It should not surprise us that Naples, a community that appreciates and admires excellent community healthcare, rallied to our distress and call for help.

This community, led capably by the physicians, put together vast resources to confront the constantly changing threat.

🔧 LEADERSHIP TOOL KIT (AMANDA)
ALERT STAKEHOLDERS

Too often, many organizations consider marketing, PR, and community relations an afterthought. Such effort quickly gets put to the side in the face of looming problems. Unfortunately, however, this strategy never works and can confuse community members. With little effort to illuminate decisions, it flies in the face of alert citizens with such an expectation. The unspoken community reaction usually results in: *Let us know some serious details about your decisions so we can make an informed judgment about whether we will choose you to take care of us.*

We paused, pivoted, and planned.

Our agency participated in the decision-making about recruiting a new leader, kept the community up to date on progress, and prepared the ground for the new leader.

Our chronicle takes you inside the crisis, exploring the cultural mandates we needed to create. We show how the board of trustees bravely grappled with the disruption and quickly shaped the solutions necessary to rescue the situation.

🔧 LEADERSHIP TOOL KIT (PAUL)
LISTEN. LEARN. LEAD.

Our method for identifying how to serve Collier County best was a simple three-step process:

- Listen to the needs of their employees and community members.
- Learn how their activities have impacted the community.
- Lead from a place of empathy and understanding.

The leadership team should leverage the perspectives of those around them when making decisions, especially when facing the unexpected. Our actions have consequences, and by examining how they've impacted our communities, we can make better decisions in the future. By embracing the cycle of listening to learn to lead, we can shape our leadership style to meet the current moment.

Then the pandemic hit.

COVID-19 arrived, and we were unsure. We were uncertain how to treat it, its virulence, how bad this would get, whether we had enough protective gear and whether a vaccine would be developed. Our heroes stepped up and leaned into their training.

Our journey takes you inside our hospitals to the doctors and nurses grappling with the worst global pandemic in the past century. We get a deeper look than we have seen on the evening news, and we may all leave this experience *not the same*. Healthcare is *not the same*. The emotional toll on our caregivers can be seen on their faces. Like soldiers returning from combat, they are *not the same*.

How can community healthcare leaders stand against challenges that bring global systems to their knees? In these crises, we look to our leaders for security and reliable information from an honest perspective. In Naples, providers who were once distanced and aloof became vital partners and learned to stay that way. We endured all this, accomplishing dramatic change, holding tight to our vision, and our posture of trusted leadership emerging from the crises. It was difficult, and our deployed strategies were not tested under such stress. What changed? Almost everything.

There are business lessons here for community leaders around the nation. In a word, authentic best describes NCH's deliberate approach throughout these back-to-back crises. We put thoughtful, precise messaging together for each community audience and created cohesive, competent community networks to lead us through this catastrophe.

With inspiring stories of leadership and teamwork, we share how crisis management and crisp communications on a regular basis played a strategic role in informing and supporting the community through a leadership transition and later when tragedy struck like lightning.

The silver lining of the pandemic has been that it has brought out a new level of devotion, community partnership, trust, and respect for our healthcare team and mission. We all became more appreciative of our community healthcare organization, our place of refuge, and the team who will risk everything to be there for us. We all need a much more open line of communication from our healthcare organization than ever before, especially when we are scared.

We documented how creating a new covenant with the doctors, hospital staff, and the community awakened what we believe has become a new day for healthcare in America.

25

We stood ready to seize this opportunity to reshape a good organization into a great organization and rebrand following the pandemic. Expectations were high on all sides.

Southwest Florida's consumers were not fooling around here. They expected world-class care from a united medical community, pulling together into partnerships and properly equipped to defeat the invader. Those who have survived the pandemic report a growing faith in a personal relationship with their trusted healers and hospital.

The next plague of the dark visitor should be met head-on differently.

+ + +

As we narrate this fascinating story, we leave behind a tool kit for such situations. We highlighted the best tactics of branding, listening, collaboration, and devotion to mission, as well as sharing leadership lessons, transparency, courage, resiliency, listening, team building, and community coalitions. We documented how creating a new covenant with the doctors, hospital staff, and the community awakened what we believe has become a new day for healthcare in America.

As Naples and Collier County dealt with the horror of the surging pandemic, witness the heroes. They are not just in the hospital. They are first responders, business leaders, restaurateurs, staff in doctor offices, and hardworking people. Seeing the power of combining transparent, community-driven leadership with inspirational high-ground marketing and communications was rewarding. Together with the City of Naples and Lee Health, we targeted mask aversion, elevated our heroes, and fought immunization resistance.

And who took on the role of shining a spotlight on all these heroes? The hospitals. Then, the hospital and the City. Then, there is the hospital, the city, and every business leader and healthcare provider in the region, assisted by the news media, who were just as frightened as all of us.

People needed information immediately. Live. Online. Total community access. How many COVID-19 patients do you have? Are they in the ICU? How are you treating this? How many are on ventilators? How many have died? What age are the victims? Had they been vaccinated? What are the doctors saying? Can we visit loved ones? What vaccines can we get and when? Should we wear masks? What symptoms are you seeing? Where can I get a test?

In this cauldron of chaos, we tested the total involvement of skilled communications during organizational decision-making. In the past, like most businesses, hospitals in America followed the traditional notion of communicating with the public after the decisions were rendered. But now, we sense that total involvement by communications professionals and a no-surprises philosophy in making the big decisions could impact a community in fear.

It was our finest hour. Trust casts sparkle over everything in a healthcare organization.

The Three-Legged Stool of American Hospitals

Before the Revolutionary War, a respected physician and a bold community leader forged a new bond between citizens and their government.

Benjamin Franklin and his good friend Dr. Thomas Bond created the nation's first hospital in 1751 in Philadelphia. About fifteen thousand people lived in Philly at the time.

Franklin promised the assembly that he would personally raise half of the funds necessary for Pennsylvania Hospital. He did so, and Lieutenant Governor Alexander Hamilton signed the bill, perhaps unaware they were setting the blueprint to develop hospitals for a nation. This historic hospital still thrives, a magnet for excellence today.[3]

At first, government legislators resisted the idea of being involved in healthcare, especially paying for it. Franklin's sixth sense about society can be described as genius.

Franklin led his new nation on instinct and intuition. In this case, he knew that the only way they could be sure to put together an effective community hospital was to form a bond of partnership between the government, the organization, and the community and keep it there.

This three-legged stool of the community hospital survived the test of time. Remove any of the three, and the stool will collapse.

---

3   Penn Medicine, History of Pennsylvania Hospital, "The Story of the Creation of the Nation's First Hospital," accessed September 1, 2021, https://www.uphs.upenn.edu/paharc/features/creation.html.

PART 1

—

EMERGING PROBLEMS

CHAPTER 1

GETTING ORGANIZED

For a hospital organization, word-of-mouth reputation and trust in the community enable robust growth. Usually, people select a hospital in a hurry, so folks have already considered their preferences before needing the service. A trusted "brand" leads to loyal patients, which leads to a more prosperous hospital, which leads to solid recruitment, great doctors joining the staff, and high-quality care.

I arrived in Naples several months before the new CEO, Paul Hiltz, arrived. I was engaged to lead the administrative transition from a PR/Comms perspective for NCH.

IS THIS HEAVEN?

The beauty of this community and the pleasant vibe of the town did not reveal that anything would be amiss in this paradise. Everything shines like new. City staff clean the streets every morning. Pleasant people cheerfully open their retail stores and restaurants. Intersections are landscaped. Buildings are color coordinated. Brand-new model cars quietly and politely traverse the town.

At the impressive NCH Downtown Baker Hospital, people smile and say hello. If you are lost, an employee will figure that out and offer to help. Construction goes on everywhere around downtown Naples. Beautiful schools, pristine track-and-field facilities, playing fields, inspiring churches, and never-ending beaches. Blue sky. Wow.

During 2018, a cascade of good news:

- The financial stability of NCH before the community protest was good. Fitch, one of the two bond rating agencies, upgraded NCH to AA.
- The Centers for Medicare & Medicaid Services awarded both NCH Baker Downtown Hospital and NCH North Naples Hospital a five-star rating.
- For the third consecutive year, Southwest Florida was named the healthiest and happiest Metropolitan Statistical Area in the nation, with the longest life expectancy that has lengthened for the second year. NCH's Blue Zones Project changed the dynamics of well-being in Southwest Florida in favor of health, happiness, and longevity.

🔧 BRANDING TOOL KIT (AMANDA)
STRATEGIC PLANNING

A strong research, data, and planning foundation is needed to craft any company's message and brand strategies. By establishing a strategic framework at the onset of any project, we ensure that an effective message reaches the market. This process ensures that we back up all our messaging and positioning with authentic facts and data. On day one, we began accumulating information and studying the organization's communications with an eye on developing a strategy to create a strong relationship with the physicians and the community.

THE JOY OF PRACTICING PRIMARY CARE

With over twelve thousand very high-income families living in the Naples region, a great demand for personalized healthcare creates a diverse and gifted group of physicians, among them many doctors who practice primary care medicine, a field that has been fighting for survival.

Lee and Collier Counties and the City of Naples have more concierge physicians than almost any other community in America. These physicians have especially deep and abiding relationships with their patients. One of our biggest mandates would be to ensure that we fully immerse these physicians in every phase of the leadership selection process.

Primary care physician surveys show frustration from our trusted healers with the pace of work. Seeing dozens of patients a day, many with very complex medical needs, work on chart detail at night, with little quality family time and compensation that needs attention.

Primary care doctors love to practice medicine and build relationships with their patients over time. Many take a close look at becoming independent concierge doctors. Their "panels" of patients are significantly smaller, and some doctors cap the number of people they will accept into their concierge practice, creating waiting lists, so to speak.

An article in *Florida Weekly, Naples Edition* by reporter Andrea Stetson reported in 2024 that patients pay a yearly fee ranging from $1,500 to $20,000 a year. In Florida, $3,000 to $6,000 a year is the more prevalent price. For that, they get more personalized care from a doctor who has fewer patients and more time to spend with each one. Concierge doctors do everything that a primary care physician would do, but also do house calls, can oversee your hospital care, coordinate with specialists, offer blood work and other tests in office, and more.[4]

A typical concierge physician has about 600 patients compared with an average panel of about 2,300 of a typical primary care physician.[5] (A patient panel refers to a group of patients assigned to one specific physician or clinical team.)

4   Andres Stetson, "Concierge Doctors," *Florida Weekly, Naples edition*, February 29, 2024, accessed May 19, 2024, https://naples.floridaweekly.com/articles/concierge-doctors/.

5   Zack Smith, "Concierge Medicine: Costs, Factors, and Considerations," Partner MD, April 27, 2023, accessed March 10, 2024, https://www.partnermd.com/blog/concierge-medicine-costs-factors-considerations.

According to recent research conducted by *Concierge Medicine Today*, a national trade publication, as many as twelve thousand physicians in the United States now operate concierge practices.[6]

Michael Tetreault, the publication's editor, notes that "generally, a concierge practice is one that charges patients an annual fee or retainer in exchange for enhanced services that aren't typically covered under traditional insurance plans. Beyond that, concierge practices can vary widely in their structure, payment requirements, and menu of services."

Practice sizes range from one hundred to one thousand patients per physician compared with three thousand or more at a traditional practice, according to Tetreault.[7]

For a typical concierge physician, the clock does not guide the care. They can go to their kids' sporting events, take vacations, and get home on time from work for dinner. Concierge physicians' spouses are thrilled with the new world order. Most importantly, talk of early retirement often stops. They love medicine again.

If that doctor delays retirement by another decade or so because they have reclaimed the joy of practicing, that softens the argument that the lighter patient panel could create a doctor shortage.

Some physicians say concierge medicine reduces the administrative burdens and costs in dealing with insurance, increases their ability to serve their patients, and improves their incomes and quality of professional life.

We have seen widespread acceptance and acclaim for concierge doctors in Southwest Florida medicine.

---

6   Janet Colwell, "Concierge Medicine Is Growing," Physicians Practice, May 16, 2016, accessed March 15, 2024, https://www.physicianspractice.com/view/concierge-medicine-growing.

7   Ibid.

Concierge physicians can pay maximum attention to the needs of their primary care patients. Open appointments, a thorough wellness focus, cell phone availability twenty-four hours a day, and unrushed clinical visits are hallmarks of this form of primary care. People pay more for this "trusted healer," a term created by the worldwide champion of primary care, Dr. Paul Grundy, international *Godfather of the Medical Home,*" to describe the perfect relationship between a patient and a healer.[8]

These influential physicians would become key players in not only preparing for the pandemic but also bringing the support of the most powerful citizens to bear on the crisis.

When it comes to seeking health aid, people have access to a variety of medical disciplines, organizations, and techniques. In today's scenario, it is possible to switch between natural cures, scientifically proven treatments, spiritual healing, and other options to cure a disease. Such medical pluralism has become a boon to modern civilization.

Another strategy to improve the experience of practicing medicine and the experience of being a primary care provider is quickly emerging worldwide in the healthcare sector.

A conference announcement for major convocations in Dubai and Las Vegas in 2024 describes the opportunity as countering a multifaceted demand:

Pluralistic health systems in 2024 is a rather debated topic, with many healthcare professionals, researchers, and policymakers actively discussing it in large-scale events.[9] Such organizations may take center stage in the coming years in primary care.

---

8   Peter B. Anderson, Bud Ramey, and Tom Emswiller, *The Familiar Physician* (New York City: Morgan James, 2014), p. xii.

9   Health 2.0 Conference, "USA Agenda 2023," 2023, accessed November 24, 2023, https://www.health2conf.com/usa-summer-2023.

"This approach offers patients a more holistic and individualized approach to healthcare and has the potential to improve health outcomes and reduce costs. But it comes with its share of challenges, the Health 2.0 conference announcement offers. A pluralistic health system is defined as one in which a variety of diverse providers, services, and organizations coexist and communicate with one another to provide healthcare to a population. For example, mixing biomedicine with 'traditional' or 'alternative' medicine to cure specific diseases."

Traditional healers, community health workers, and other nontraditional healthcare professionals are frequently included in these systems, along with both public and commercial healthcare providers. Numerous nations have pluralistic health systems (Canada, the United Kingdom, Australia), which are rapidly elevating them to the forefront of conversation at upcoming healthcare events.[10]

LEADERSHIP TOOL KIT (PAUL)
ISSUING EDICTS

An essential leadership practice cultivates the ability to bring people along without issuing edicts. That can be harder than it looks. We have found a direct connection with good listening, and that skill comes naturally to managers who practice that art. Thus, listening directly affects the organization's reputation and brand. Leadership today, no matter what you are doing, requires keeping the people with you, like a mayor would have constituents. You can't just issue edicts. You can, but it doesn't go over well.

---

10   Ibid.

Board chair Mariann MacDonald guided us to begin a thorough reputation management program within the community. As soon as we finished accessing the strength of the community relations and the employee and physician morale, our relationship could evolve into more of a marketing and branding role. The Partnership was willing to be a part of the assignment.

Things were happening fast; as soon as we arrived, new leadership would be recruited, and the doctors and the community would want to know all about the selection process.

For a hospital organization, word-of-mouth reputation and a sense of trust in the community enable robust growth. Usually, people select a hospital in a hurry, so they have already considered their preferences before they need the service.

Trust casts sparkle.

BRANDING TOOL KIT (AMANDA)
DEFINING A STRONG BRAND

Strong brand identity reaches far beyond logos and taglines—it guides your audience's emotional responses and embodies your business entirely. We believe a meaningful, well-established brand look and feel sets the tone for all marketing activities. Our insights group uncovers unique communication options, which allows our team to craft messaging platforms and plans that are purpose-built to create belonging. You never stop working on your brand. Even in a disruption, the team advances ideas about future branding efforts.

We mused over the times we live in. We have seen an unsettled culture in America: racial equity demonstrations, police protests, a polarized society politically, racially, spiritually, school board meetings turning nasty, elections questioned, increased violence, and mistrust of news media. Every aspect of our culture has been on edge. Has a new day of total openness arrived in healthcare? What about the fragility of the doctor-hospital relationships everywhere?

+ + +

Our doctors, and most especially our concierge physicians, wanted a say in who would be selected to run their healthcare organization. There had been conflict in Naples regarding the employment of hospitalists in the hospitals. So, the leadership of NCH faced dissension by the concierge physicians who felt they were being pushed out of caring for their patients.

For the last several decades, hospitals have been buying up as many practices as they can afford, hoping to create predictable patterns of inpatient admissions and referrals to their network. (Many of these physician organizations have not yet discovered how to operate this strategy without losing money.) Most physicians have been independent business owners for their entire career. But those doctors who choose to become healthcare system employees, while not having to fret over as many administrative drains on their time, have other complaints. They often say they have little or no say in the organization's direction.

Some health systems have such a strong balance sheet that they shrug off the cost of operating the primary care network as a necessary growth expense. Others are shocked at the annual financial losses.

Many citizens feel that their trusted healer, their family doctor, connects them to the puzzling world of healthcare. If they get mad at the hospital, they go to their doctor, the news media, or members of the board of trustees.

🔧 PR TOOL KIT (AMANDA)
SOMETIMES YOU JUST HAVE TO ASK

In new leadership situations, you frequently have little time to scan for problematic events in the past. We learned that the NCH System Summer of 2018 split with the highly beloved Neighborhood Health Clinic was a pain still being felt in the community. We had not heard much about this in the community dialogue. But when asked about it, citizens got fired up. Sometimes, just ask.

In a new role, or when faced with a crisis, being curious helps solve problems and move faster. Ask questions. What-ifs and curious questions can lead to new insights. And now we discovered there were some other issues beneath the surface. That quiet separation from the Neighborhood Health Clinic left some scars. Hundreds of devoted doctors and nurses in the community volunteered there. The clinic accepts zero government funding. Donors and caregivers love to support the health needs of Naples' weakest and most vulnerable citizens. They do so on their own time, which exemplifies a key part of the Benjamin Franklin/Thomas Bond concept of a community hospital. Citizens helped where they could. They created a place where the weakest, frailest, and most needy can go for help.

To their credit, the Neighborhood Health Clinic's leadership made little protest about the separation from the NCH organization. But loyal volunteers watched and were not happy.

The *Naples Daily News* reported that the Neighborhood Health Clinic falling-out with the NCH may have had a silver lining.[11]

The newspaper noted that philanthropic residents who were curtailing donations to NCH were boosting financial support to the clinic and similar causes, said Dolph von Arx, another past chairman of the NCH board.

People will double down their support to the Neighborhood Health Clinic, von Arx said.

Nancy Lascheid, cofounder of the clinic with her late husband, said there were signs that was occurring. The clinic was seeing an increase in new donations.[12]

Neighborhood Health Clinic, opened in 1999, offers a medical home to working residents of Collier County who are uninsured, or have little coverage, so they could get regular care in a dignified manner. Patients must meet qualification guidelines to be treated at the clinic. That means they often can forgo waits in emergency rooms that drive up costs for hospitals. So, enlightened self-interest motivates most hospitals to strongly champion neighboring free clinics.

In addition, Neighborhood Health Clinic serves residents of St. Matthew's House, the homeless shelter with a structured program for people to get back on their feet.

Mariann MacDonald noted years later that the administration did not handle the clinic issue well at all, and that was a regret.

---

11   Liz Freeman, "Neighborhood Health Clinic May Benefit from Falling-Out with NCH System," *Naples Daily Press*, January 12, 2019, accessed March 10, 2024, https://www.naplesnews.com/story/news/health/2019/01/12/neighborhood-health-clinic-may-see-silver-lining-cuts-nch/2550620002/.

12   Ibid.

However, in the hierarchy of concerns, it fell way below the radar when compared with the hospitalists' flashpoint in the community.

🔧 BRANDING TOOL KIT (AMANDA)
TRUST AND STORYTELLING

Achieving trust opens the gateway to creativity in communications. Without it, your stories and your narrative about the organization may lack authenticity. Built on a strong strategic foundation, a great creative team seeks the unexpected to build a true and lasting sense of belonging through the art of storytelling. Ideation, design, and copy all work closely together to provide authentic collateral design. But the message must be real, truthful, and indisputable. Listen closely to the people around you. Authentic stories will emerge. Your brand will evolve.

We all know that decisions made by leadership may take years to impact the organization's reputation and brand. If there is even a slight loss of trust, it cascades like throwing a pebble in a pond. When the water is calm, it has a flat surface. By throwing the pebble in, concentric circles of disruption emanate outward to the shore. Dissolving the relationship with the clinic without community discussion was like heaving a rock into that pond.

Vann Ellison, president and chief executive officer of St. Matthew's House, observed that when a nonprofit like NCH moves away from its purpose of serving the needs of the community and the less fortunate, it starts to look like "big business," and that's unfortunate.

In January 2019, NCH responded to the controversy by reminding people that "This past fiscal year, NCH has provided more than $170 million in charity care and uncompensated care for individuals in our community. In today's ever-changing environment it is essential that we provide healthcare services in the most efficient and effective manner possible."[13]

The *Naples Daily News* reported that the clinic has just a handful of employees; the rest are volunteers, including 250 physicians, 150 nurses, and 250 support staff. They all are protected by sovereign immunity from medical malpractice, and that protection continued when a physician at the clinic referred patients to NCH for specialty treatment, John Cardillo, the clinic's attorney, told elected leaders at a Collier County Commission meeting.

So, the leadership of the organization had, in the minds of many physicians and hundreds of others, stopped listening.

Ringing up sales in the NCH North Naples Hospital Gift Shop, devoted 1,500-hour volunteer Sherry Clauson paused from her work to describe the community uprising. It had been over two years since the separation of NCH from the clinic.

"As time goes by," Sherry said, "people change, the world gets bigger, the world changes." Sherry, who has worked at both hospitals for two decades before becoming a steady volunteer, got a bit emotional and gathered her thoughts for a moment.

"The clinic … the Neighborhood Clinic …," she added, "they walked away from it. That was the biggest mistake. This was a community hospital, and that's what it thrived on for years. So yeah, it wasn't a good thing."

"We felt that our magnanimity and community service was gone."

---

13   Liz Freeman, "Neighborhood Health Clinic May Benefit from Falling-out with NCH Healthcare System," Naples Daily News, January 12, 2019, accessed September 1, 2021, https://www.naplesnews.com/story/news/health/2019/01/12/neighborhood-health-clinic-may-see-silver-lining-cuts-nch/2550620002/.

As he looks back on it, Dr. Bryan Murphey, then interim chief medical officer for NCH, agreed there may be something to the theory that the pot was already on the stove when the NCH CEO walked away from the Neighborhood Clinic without warning, which set the stage for the severity of the hospitalist crisis.

"There very well may be something to that," he noted. "The CEO explained the split because the clinic was claiming charity care being done by NCH."

NCH

NCH Mission:

Helping everyone live a longer, happier, and healthier life

NCH Core Value:

Excellence in every patient experience

Our team gradually took stock of the efforts of the two hospitals to communicate internally and externally. It was time to build a louder community voice to heal past wounds.

PR TOOL KIT (AMANDA)
ZERO SPIN

When you neglect your brand, you have no marketing communications, and in the absence of all that, someone will tell your story for you. Your words matter. No comment conveys guilt.

If you don't tell your story, someone else will. Reporters complained that there needed to be better mutual confidence and understanding between the organization and the media. This was a perfect case study of what happens when you don't tell your story and give the media enough information to build an accurate narrative. Under most circumstances, respond to every press inquiry immediately, with accurate information and zero spin. Build relationships and be a resource.

BLUE RIBBONS VERSUS IMPOLITE POSTERS

Events took a turn on Tuesday, January 22, 2019, when two competing rallies were held just before noon in Naples: one with blue ribbons of support, the other with banners, protest signs, and chanting.

At the city's Cambier Park, over 150 citizens attended. This expansive, lovely green space and sporting event park lies right in the heart of downtown Naples, just south of the prestigious Fifth Avenue South. Frequently big band sounds or jazz from the concert shell can be heard by guests at the outdoor cafes lining the shopping district.

On this day, there was a protest against the hospital leadership. Moving and emotional testimony by key physicians and passionate citizens led the crowd into a rally of high moral seriousness. Broadcast media and newspaper reporters were there to record it.[14]

---

14   Liz Freeman, "Yard Signs Spread," *Naples Daily News*, December 2, 2019, accessed September 1, 2021, https://www.naplesnews.com/story/news/health/2018/12/02/ yard-signs-spread-naples-area-vs-nch-limits-doctors-hospital-use/2154905002/.

Simultaneously, NCH employees organized a rally in support of the hospital.[15]

More than two hundred blue ribbons of support were handed out to employees as they streamed outside NCH Downtown Baker Hospital to the pavilion at the meditative, shady Garden of Hope and Courage on the campus. The administration stated at the rally that "We have been here sixty-three years, and we will be here another sixty-three years doing what we do best, taking care of patients."

"My heart is so full right now. I'm happy to see every one of you," Christina Carranza, an NCH employee who helped organize the rally, said to the group. She said they started organizing the rally four days before the event, using #StandWithNCH.

---

15 Liz Freeman, "NCH Employees Rally in Support of CEO, While Doctors and Others Protest in Cambier Park," *Naples Daily News*, January 22, 2019, accessed September 1, 2021, https://www.naplesnews.com/story/news/health/2019/01/22/rallies-both-sides-nch-debate-each-draw-crowds-hospital-cambier-park/2643233002/.

Former Naples City Council members, among dozens of other community leaders,[16] attended the Cambier Park protest rally to support independent physicians in the community and hear what the community was saying.[17]

Bryan Murphey, MD, had served as a hospitalist with the Cleveland Clinic in Ohio and New York when they operated a hospital in Naples. He built their hospitalist program and recruited hospitalists, so he had deep experience with this. Four clinical and administrative team members ventured out into the community to answer questions and explain the pilot program. At that time, many people did not know what a hospitalist was.

"I was part of three community presentations to try to explain the program," he recalled.

"The disruption was very difficult," Dr. Murphey recalled.

"It was very upsetting to the town and the physicians. We clearly heard that.[18] The CEO did not want the community primary care physicians to be able to place orders on the patients initially. He wanted the hospitalist team to take care of the patients solely, and then later, as the outrage grew,[19] he pivoted to co-management, but at that point, it was a little bit too late," Dr. Murphey said.

---

16   Jack Lowenstein, "Former NCH Board Members Urge Hospital to Reconsider," WINK-TV News, December 7, 2018, accessed September 1, 2021, https://www.winknews.com/2018/12/07/former-nch-board-members-urge-hospital-to-reconsider-patient-policy/.

17   "Yard Signs in Naples Protest NCH Policy Change," Fox4News, December 4, 2018, accessed September 1, 2021, https://www.youtube.com/watch?v=qCOJ1lyWl-8.

18   Liz Freeman, "Healthcare Faces Legal Threat," *Naples Daily News*, December 11, 2018, accessed March 11, 2024, https://www.naplesnews.com/story/news/health/2018/12/11/nch-healthcare-faces-legal-threat-if-admissions-policy-change-isnt-dropped/2274793002/.

19   Jack Lowenstein, "Former NCH Board Members Urge Hospital to Reconsider," WINK-TV News, July 12, 2018, accessed March 11, 2024, https://www.winknews.com//former-nch-board-members-urge-hospital-to-reconsider-patient-policy/.

"I'm not entirely clear why he wanted it 'closed' to community physicians. We are a community hospital. And when you're a community hospital, you're a community hospital. It should be open to the community physicians and patients to select who they want to care for them."

Dr. Murphey wrote an Opinion piece with the local newspaper urging everyone to calm down. He was a voice of reason in a growing storm.[20]

The administration submitted a guest editorial to the *Naples Daily News* to answer questions regarding the hospitalist program and ask for patience in assessing its performance. But while the newspapers were whirling off the press, everything changed.[21]

The next day, Wednesday, January 23, 2019, the NCH board unanimously accepted the resignation of the CEO and chief of staff. A highly regarded administrative team member was immediately selected as interim administrator.

Dr. Murphey later observed that the CEO did not listen to his community, so it was indeed time to move on. That's not what a community hospital is all about.

"A community hospital must listen to its community," he said.

---

20   Liz Freeman, "NCH Sticking to Hospital Admissions Change, Plan," *Naples Daily News*, December 13, 2018, accessed September 1, 2021, https://www.naplesnews.com/story/news/health/2018/12/13/nch-tries-appease-outcry-over-admissions.

21   "NCH Medical Staff Vote to Remove CEO and COS," WINK-TV News, January 17, 2019, accessed September 1, 2021, https://www.winknews.com/2019/01/17/nch-medical-staff-vote-to-remove-ceo-and-cos/.

🛠 BRANDING TOOL KIT (AMANDA)
PAUSE AND REFLECT

For a few hours, all was quiet. This was a moment of self-reflection. It was halftime. We have a great team of The Partnership pros engaged. Our diverse expertise has been designed for just this kind of situation: public relations professionals with experience building an organization's reputation through digital and traditional media. Our process includes analyzing, finding positive messages, and translating those messages into impactful media stories. Next, our team will organize brand building, crisis communications, and media training. We will seek to work closely with the media to tell the NCH story as it unfolds in the days ahead. But at this moment, we needed some contemplation.

What It Means to Be a Community Hospital
By Bill Barker

Bill Barker served as president and publisher of the Naples Daily News *for seven years, guiding the journalistic coverage of the leadership change at NCH and through the pandemic.*

Their intentions were not bad. The health system administrators cared about the healthcare organization's reputation, and they felt very strongly that they had a map to bring better care to our community. Collaboration was not too far of a stretch.

The administration was just determined that they knew the right approach, and they stuck to that until, basically, they couldn't put the toothpaste back in the tube.

That's ultimately, in my opinion, where that fell apart.

Naples has evolved into a highly intellectual and engaged community with good discernment. For a town the size of Naples, there are probably more retired college presidents and CEOs concentrated in this community than anywhere else in the country. They can make good judgment with quality information on what's in their best interest. That was, to me, a "miss" on the past administration, not believing that people could maneuver and get involved in a dispute when they built this hospital from their own funds and their own resources for the purpose of this community.

In my mind, the administration always has a dual responsibility: one to the patient outcomes as the stewards of that healthcare organization and equally to the community that built it. That community has a voice, and that voice needs to be heard. From my observation, the thing that was the most troubling was that they were not listening to such a strong voice.

CHAPTER 2

STRATEGY AND STRUCTURE

Over the months, because of community input, changes at NCH occurred in our voluntary board leadership. Right after the resignations of the previous administration, at the February 2019 meeting, our board of trustees added two longtime business and philanthropic leaders in the community: Jay Baker and Scott Lutgert.

Mariann MacDonald recalls the moments before and after the board voted to remove the administration.

"I reached out to two of the most vocal community leaders, Scott Lutgert and Jay Baker. They had written me a letter expressing deep concerns about NCH leadership," Mariann recalled.

It was instrumental to have them, she noted.

"I said, come in and be a part of the new board. Come help me and let me understand what we need to do."

Mariann had served for ten years as board chair and was very pleased that they agreed to be part of the solution. As her retirement neared, she was lining up key leaders to help reshape the board's direction and to demonstrate to everyone that it was a new day at NCH.

Changes in board leadership occur at the annual meeting, and it was very timely since the new members would be able to participate in the new leadership search.

"I vividly recall their reaction once they signed on and learned the full story of what was happening at NCH," she added.

"We already had board members Michael Wynn and Kevin Beebe, who were both fantastic people," Mariann recalled. "Greg Russo, Tom Gazdic, and Dr. John Lewis were all scheduled to change over at the upcoming annual meeting, and so was I."

So now was the time to bring in the most powerful leadership we could, with some of the best business leadership and experience in the region, especially with a national search about to begin for a new president.

Shortly after Paul arrived in December 2019, three more leaders were added: Alan Einhorn, William Perez, and Davey Scoon. These additions were the result of community input—Mariann's goal of having a fully staffed and functional board in place before her retirement was met.

Mariann MacDonald's departure was understandable but difficult for us. Inspirational and incredibly knowledgeable, she was in her tenth year of service at NCH. A visionary and an operational engineer, she worked in pharmaceuticals most of her career. She worked for DuPont for thirty years in top management, arranging a management buyout that included several mainstream products, including the highly successful products Percocet and Percodan. Her company, Endo Pharmaceuticals, became a powerhouse.

Mariann MacDonald, former chairman of the board, NCH

Mariann created our Children's ER and funded many other projects. She was vital in getting us up and running at NCH. We celebrated her decade-long role as board chair and the other retiring members, publishing her long list of accomplishments and recognizing her devotion to her community.

NCH named Scott Lutgert as the new chair, to take the helm on March 30, 2020. Scott has been unwavering in supporting the Naples and Southwest Florida community. He was previously on the board of directors of Naples Community Hospital from 2001 to 2009. In 2015, he and his wife Simone chaired the Magnolia Ball supporting the NCH William and Susan Dalton Oncology Unit. With his bachelor's degree from Stanford University and an MBA from the University of Chicago, Scott's commitment to education and healthcare is a source of pride. Since 1970, he has been a major force in the social fabric of Southwest Florida and a leading citizen in Naples and Collier County.

The next task Mariann tackled was bringing in a solid communications expert. That's when The Partnership put boots on the ground and began evaluating the public relations crisis.

"Amanda came in, and that made a big difference," Mariann later recalled. "Amanda reminded us that it is not just business, especially in healthcare, but relationships between the customer and the organization and how you build that trust."

The fading echoes of the public rallies became the soundtrack for the following events. Within a few days of our arrival in Naples, the NCH board of trustees engaged a national search firm to recruit a new CEO. The NCH board asked my team at The Partnership to lead all internal and external (or public) communications and to be a crucial part of the search for new leadership. It would be months before a new CEO would step in. Transparency would rule.

Our agency experience has been to help create partnerships with purpose and passion for economic development, healthcare, retail ventures, and consumer packaged goods. We have created an iconic entertainment district in Atlanta. Our deep experience in branding has helped many organizations become national players. We worked with governments and politicians. We started to carefully lay the groundwork for building their community voice.

The board of trustees interviewed the international search firm Russell Reynolds Associates to recruit a new CEO, carefully testing the waters with physicians and community leaders. They received solid endorsements from key community leaders such as Bob Stucker, whose international business acumen has brought him close contact with the firm on several occasions. A search committee was chosen with influential physician leaders.

Letting the dust settle, the board publicly announced the search in March 2019. The trustees asked me to meet with and learn from the physicians who are so important to the organization.

Dr. Paul Jones

The current president of the medical staff was Paul O. Jones, MD, PA, and we made time for many lunch breaks during the weeks before the CEO selection. Deeply respected, he operates a thriving concierge practice. He is very empathetic; people join a waiting list to have him as their trusted healer. On his website, he notes that the concierge practice allows doctors to reduce the number of patients they see "by at least 80 percent, providing optimum personal attention to every patient."

Dr. Jones emerged as a key leader in instrumenting this change.

Dr. Jim Mahon

Dr. Jim Mahon, senior vice president for philanthropy, recalled Dr. Jones's epic role in the NCH story.

"Dr. Paul Jones represents our Mother Teresa. I mean, he is a Mother Teresa. He still has scars from the management disruption. He's just the kindest man and a great doctor. He's an important part of the NCH history and a very important part of our present."

Dr. Jones would have a lead role in selecting the new CEO.

The team from Russell Reynolds began planning the national search. We started understanding NCH's long and respected history, a six-month disciplined observation.

The search firm began their own fact-finding and listening. They conducted focus groups to receive input from the community, and we were invited. The team also conducted interviews all over the region.

After several weeks they developed a profile of the skill sets of the executive they would seek. Perhaps the most important excerpt from this lengthy document was on leadership:

Leadership/Behavioral Criteria

- Have significant credibility based on experience and reputation in healthcare delivery and organizational transformation.
- Show an ability for strong leadership with outstanding relationship and communication skills built on a foundation of transparency.
- Be an entrepreneurial thinker who embraces change with an ability to build partnerships to achieve shared goals.
- Show the ability to effectively balance decisiveness and collaboration to achieve positive results.
- Be a team/relationship builder who can unify all stakeholders around mission and goals.
- Show ability to set tone and example, building a culture that inspires organizational, team, and individual excellence.
- Demonstrate balance between optimism and realism by being highly strategic while also successfully executing.

Meanwhile, in Ohio, Paul Hiltz, a candidate for the next CEO of NCH, was contemplating the final chapter of his forty-year career in healthcare.

Russell Reynolds made a telephone call.

Americans want to trust their providers. We naturally gravitate toward supporting our community hospital. We want to have a trusted healer. We intuitively feel that the community leg of the stool cannot be disrespected. Physicians are a huge piece of that community.

The Partnership team moved through Naples, listening carefully.

🔧 LEADERSHIP TOOL KIT (PAUL)
SPEAKING OUT

The human nature of organizations suggests that when a vacuum exists at the top, it makes it the time to stand up for your piece of the whole. People finally become eager to speak out about their views of things. The physicians and employees who spoke openly and honestly to us reported that they are wishful for a more inclusive culture. This was the most frequent comment we heard.

Many citizens wanted to be involved here in Naples and Collier County. Just changing the administrative management was not enough. Their issues with the healthcare system stem from a deep desire for collaboration and listening, and the new boss had not arrived yet to show us that it *would be a different day.*

🔧 LEADERSHIP TOOL KIT (PAUL)
PROBLEM-SOLVING

How do you shift a culture like that? The new CEO will need to set new leadership expectations throughout the organization. Albert Einstein once said, "No problem can be solved from the same level of consciousness that created it." It appeared that our pending leadership change would do well to apply that advice.

Most hospital boards seek a reputation for their community healthcare organization that's a "for the people, by the people" kind of thing. Community healthcare needs the guidance of a board of directors with significant leadership and business acumen. Their friends, business colleagues, and neighbors reach out to them when things are not right. These leaders also want their organization to be a growth institution. Every business leader has the DNA to reach for broader impact, and in healthcare, that means being a part of growing the organization into clinical excellence and embracing evidence-based medicine.

Board members know the importance of a branding and marketing effort, having robust communications inside and outside the organization, and having a high-ground message that places the community first.

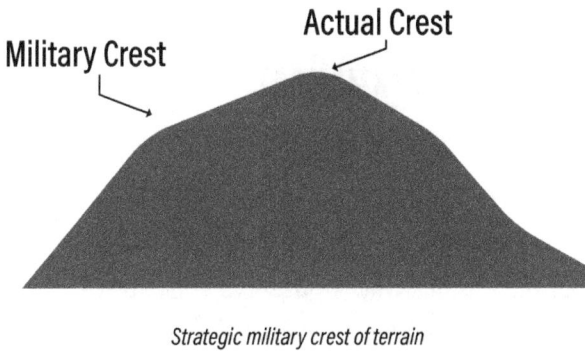

Strategic military crest of terrain

If we consider changing situations strategically through the lens of our military leaders, every organization, consciously or unconsciously, seeks to occupy the highest possible terrain.

But not the very top of a hill, which would be vulnerable to observation and fire from all points of the compass. The "military crest" resides just below that height, usually affording better cover. It is not an easy target from below, but you can still observe. And listen.[22] We were planning to relocate to the "military crest," the most defensive position we could take, which was to base our communications on one primary statement, which no one can dispute: "Helping everyone live a longer, happier, and healthier life."

The people who work in our hospitals take pride in their contribution to healing. Right now, we all want to feel like we stand on *high ground.* First and foremost, we must remind the five thousand stakeholders in NCH that we value their work as powerful, meaningful, worthy, and appreciated. Looking back at this brief plan, we are proud that we focused on the *high ground* and the noble purpose we all shared. This goes without saying anytime in healthcare, especially now, on the eve of new leadership.

PR TOOL KIT (AMANDA)
RESPECT THE DEEP HISTORY

From this moment on, our "deep history" should be the first words out of our mouths. It's why we deserve your trust. These cannot be just words. It must be a continuation of a long-made promise. It must be sincere. It must be about community, about promises for openness that people want and need. We need to remind the people of the region that we have been earning their trust for decades. We have been, and always will be, the leading hospital in the area for everyone.

We knew for sure that community trust could be achieved. We can enhance the bond between the healthcare organization and its

---

22   American Battlefield Trust, "A Glossary of Fortification Terms," accessed March 11, 2024, https://www.battlefields.org/learn/articles/glossary-fortification-terms.

citizens. It may take a while. And we must earn it. This community was in watchful waiting for their new healthcare leader to come.

As the first new soldiers on the ground, NCH doctors studied us with the same glare as Customs agents in the airport, determining if they could trust us … or not. After a while, they probably decided that at least we had no banned agricultural products or counterfeit goods.

Were we representing the old viewpoints? Or heralding the new?

A short while after the resignations, the hospitalist physicians of NCH listened to a proposal from Dr. Sajan Rao, chairman of the internal medicine department, to form a new task force of representatives of all the hospitalist groups and independent concierge physicians at NCH.

This task force met weekly to develop the criteria and performance metrics of a new CEO. Their stated priority was continued excellent care for the residents and visitors of Southwest Florida. Meanwhile, our communications team began developing a plan to help the organization overcome this crisis. Looking back on the initial efforts to begin the healing process, this initial plan served us well. It set up a sincere and solid framework for where we were to go from this point.

We entitled our plan "Serving a larger story."

We knew we must address the attack on NCH core values.

"Community," a very powerful word for NCH, holds the strength and confidence of focused local attention. It supports the full story of the best hospital in the area that has always been ingrained and dedicated to the local community.

That was written in the eye of the storm. But vocal leaders asked for transparency in selecting a new CEO and offering suggestions about where to go from here. They hoped the new leadership would arrive and share the keys to the house. So, after every heartbeat of watchful waiting, we embarked on a period of what, in hindsight, looks a bit like overcommunication.

In early February 2019, we saw some daylight after an all-in focus on press and media relations, trying to manage the media requests about the management change. We began with employees, which included written communication and internal town hall meetings with staff and volunteers.

PR TOOL KIT (AMANDA)
POSITIVE DEVELOPMENTS

Our communications team developed a continuous flow of positive news about NCH. Positive developments can become like rungs on a ladder. Even small victories, when published back-to-back over time, indicate a trend. This also fills the awkward silence. During the summer, we featured blogs, newsletters, social posts, and web banners featuring the work of the patient-centered care task force, the physicians' wellness program and physicians' retreat, quality care and patient-first philosophy, the Simulation Center, the neuro-stroke program, the cardiac surgery program, joint replacement center awards, the new PACS system, and ultimately, the new CEO and his vision of transparency and collaboration.

NCH expanded the board of trustees with two more civic and philanthropic leaders, an action described in our press release "in recognition of the need to expand our membership and partnership with the community."

In addition, the medical executive committee of the NCH medical staff unanimously voted to reinstate Paul Jones, MD, as president of the medical staff. On April 5, the *Naples Daily News* published an interview with Cesar De Leon, MD, president of the Collier County Medical Society, who said that the community needs information.

"It will be helpful. We want to know who they are. Don't keep it a secret."[23]

Separately, the newspaper added that the executive search firm was interviewing various civic and business leaders for feedback. The search was expected to span three to four months, and Collier Commissioner Penny Taylor said having the names of the search committee would be helpful to the community.[24]

The news writers seemed to accept the response that more information on the search will be released later, but not now. Community leaders who are taking part in the interviews seem content. But many were tapping their feet.

Dr. De Leon was among the NCH's executive medical committee members who spoke with Russell Reynolds representatives about qualities they desired in a new CEO. The meetings were not one-on-one with the search firm, which Dr. De Leon did not see as necessary since those present were like-minded. If any of them asked for private meetings, he believed the search firm would accommodate that. The

---

23 R. Lynn Wilson, "Guest Commentary: Former Healthcare Executive Offers His Advice to NCH," *Naples Daily News*, February 15, 2019, accessed September 1, 2021, https://www.naplesnews.com/story/opinion/2019/02/15/former-healthcare-executive-offers-advice-nch/2815394002/.

24 Liz Freeman, "Search for New CEO of NCH System Faces Criticism for Lack of Transparency," *Naples Daily News*, May 25, 2019, accessed September 1, 2021, https://www.naplesnews.com/story/news/health/2019/05/25/nch-keeping-community-dark-civic-watchdogs-say/3751271002/.

next CEO needs to engage with the medical staff and have a more horizontal management structure.[25]

Some community leaders whom the search firm contacted included Naples mayor Bill Barnett.

"So far, I think they get the idea."

The *Naples Daily News* also interviewed a former NCH CEO to listen to his reaction.

"It's important the search firm and the committee reach out to a variety of people in the community to make sure their needs are taken into account," said Edward Morton, former CEO of NCH, who stepped down in 2006. He insisted on the involvement of Hispanic citizens. Morton also voiced the need to improve relationships with charities and other healthcare providers. He referred to Lee Health, the public hospital system in Lee County, and Healthcare Network of Southwest Florida, which runs dozens of outpatient centers in Collier to predominantly serve disadvantaged residents.[26]

The newspaper covered the progress, reporting that "a national search for a new chief executive officer for NCH was gaining momentum, intending to offer the position to a top candidate in July."

"There are hundreds of candidates that are under consideration. Now it is down roughly thirty," the newspaper reported.

"The process is underway, with several interviews set for round two in the coming weeks."

---

25   Ibid.

26   Wilson, "Guest Commentary: Former Healthcare Executive Offers His Advice to NCH."

🔧 LEADERSHIP TOOL KIT (PAUL)
CULTURAL TURNAROUND

What does a turnaround look like? It needs to be stated that there are different kinds of turnarounds in business. Many may think turnaround means stemming the bleeding financially, righting the financial ship, and bringing the organization back to sustainability. But cultural collapse can happen for a host of reasons. The internal audience often no longer feels a part of the organization. They have been left out of the equation, and no one watches out for their interests.

They are no longer brand believers.

Such a loss of loyalty spreads to the consumers within whispering distance (like doctors and patients), which impacts the brand, which can be described as essentially the sum of the loyalty earned by the organization.

In June, we had some good news about recent advances in radiology. We created print ads, blog posts, social posts, and website banners to support the same story, using a credible community focus for all materials. In addition, the new task force of ten physicians, representing a cross-section of practice groups in Collier County, had some positive results from their five-month "patient-centered" study. The tone of the discussion was changing. Doctors were feeling more in tune with the decision-making in the hospitals. Dr. Alejandro Perez-Trepichio, chief medical officer of the group practice, said that he felt good about his participation and opportunity for input.

Dr. Joseph Repay, an independent concierge physician on the task force, said the intent is to improve patient care and make NCH a great institution. Repay said the atmosphere at NCH has improved since the administration change, but there were unknowns until a decision was made on a new CEO.

"In general, everyone is pleased."

Back in the day, NCH hospitalists would visit patients during rounds with a multidisciplinary team from rehabilitation, pharmacy, and elsewhere to improve efficiency, quality, and continuity of care. This effectively left out the independent concierge doctors, who were not employed by NCH and did not have the benefit of the multidisciplinary team to help improve their patient outcomes. That needed to change.

"This is the way it should have been done," said Dr. Zubin Pachori, a task force member.

"So far we are satisfied with how it has been open to everyone."

Then, there was a burst of white light.

We looked up. Everyone in Naples took a deep breath.

White smoke.

PART 2

ENDURING CRISES

CHAPTER 3

HOW TO BUILD TEAMS IN A CRISIS

There really wasn't white smoke.

Nor were the participants locked in, as in a conclave of the College of Cardinals. The word "conclave" comes from the Latin "with a key," as *locked with a key*. The cardinals lock the Sistine Chapel to ensure secrecy and to protect them from outside influence. But our conclave was not locked in, and we did not burn anything or ring the bells as the papal conclave does upon the selection of a new pope.

Our search committee's choice was unanimous. The bells in Naples didn't ring, but maybe they should have. There are eighty-eight historic churches in the city. The bells would have signaled a new day.[27]

---

27 Laura Layden, "NCH Chooses New CEO," *Naples Daily News*, July 26, 2019, accessed September 1, 2021, https://www.naplesnews.com/story/news/local/2019/07/26/nch-chooses-new-ceo-naples-hospital-health-care/1835962001/.

Now, our mission here evolved. The Partnership would help NCH introduce and onboard a new CEO, which includes media relations, brand and voice evolution, creative designs, and web development. We began with a beautiful campaign to introduce Paul Hiltz to the doctors, the media, the employees, the donors, the volunteers, and the community.

We flew to Ohio to produce a video so that the people could see and hear from the new CEO himself. They could get to know the person behind the title. Special events were arranged. Advance feature articles appeared in local magazines.

Kevin Beebe

"The search began with one hundred candidates," said board member Kevin Beebe. "From there, we whittled that talent pool down to eleven. Then we eliminated five candidates—the quarterfinals—

and we got it down to the semifinals with two people. Of course, Paul Hiltz was the choice."[28]

Being sensitive to the need to inform the employees, physicians, volunteers, and donors first, we spread the announcement and posted the introductory video.

On Friday, July 26, 2019, board vice chair Tom Gazdic announced the news to the doctors right away, a perfect, healing message to the medical staff audience still stewing.

"I've been involved in the community here for many years," Gazdic said, "and it's an honor to serve this hospital. NCH is at the heart of this community, and I'm constantly impressed with the great work you do. I enjoy hearing stories of how you are keeping people healthy, healing, and saving lives. It's purposeful work that deserves an exceptional leader."

"That's why I'm here today: to share that the board has unanimously selected a new CEO and president of NCH."

"In a moment, you'll have the opportunity to hear from him through a video introduction. He is experienced, credible, honest, collaborative, and desires a deep connection with our community."

Meanwhile, Paul Hiltz was in Naples visiting NCH campuses, taking part in press conferences and medical staff meetings, and attending the meet-and-greet opportunities.

---

28   Ibid.

Michael Wynn

"Mr. Hiltz's record of results exemplifies everything that NCH stands for," said Michael Wynn, a member of the NCH search committee. "When he talks about community, he means it. His commitment to physician engagement and collaborative culture will bring a new energy to our hospital system that will make us stronger."

"Paul is the perfect person to lead NCH," committee member Scott Lutgert said. "He strongly believes in collaboration and teamwork. He has the skill set to take NCH to a new level of excellence."

"We've always been active in our communities. We want to give something back wherever we go," Hiltz said. "For me and my family, this opportunity is about connections with the community, partnerships with doctors, and excellence in patient care."

🔧 LEADERSHIP TOOL KIT (PAUL)
READY. SET. GO.

We named our strategic communications process "Ready. Set. Go." because most companies Go before they're Ready and Set, costing them time and money. Our "Ready. Set. Go." process keeps that from happening. We work together as a team through proven steps that allow for more innovative thinking and easier internal and external buy-in. The tone and tenor of our communications will reflect harmony, excitement, change, evolution, and optimism. Transparent with the media, we do not parse words, dodge questions, or spin information. Our brand builds trust, the one thing indispensable to a healthcare organization.

Our team developed a comprehensive introduction for Paul Hiltz, which we deployed throughout the community. Where we had the opportunity, we used the introductory video as well.

Consultants should become immersed in the environment at the outset, learning everything possible about the challenge. The Partnership team agreed that what we found so valuable about our assignment was that we had participated in the stakeholder interviews with the search firm. The result has been a comprehensive understanding of this community and the NCH System.

The official press release was sent out to all media, helping the citizens understand the background and intent of this new leadership and offering a sense of belonging to the community.

We'll be as involved in this community
as you'll let us be.

—PAUL HILTZ

Introducing Paul Hiltz

Hiltz prides himself on his ability to collaborate. He's bringing his C's approach to Naples.

The first C, the Community, is paramount for Hiltz and wife, Kris. The couple has been part of Ohio's community nonprofits and charitable organizations throughout his career. And when they arrive on the white sandy beaches of Naples, the community can expect more of the same.

"We're all about community," said Hiltz to the staff at Naples Community Hospital on August 1.

"We love the notion of getting to know people here, getting to know a faith community. From your Blue Zones project, we know that being part of a community is good for all of us—it's good for our health and our longevity."

Kris Hiltz has a heart for philanthropy and spends her career serving others.

"Just giving back and learning what different organizations need and helping them find extra people to work with them," said Kris Hiltz. "I hear that there are a lot of organizations that have volunteers. I want to make sure that all the organizations have enough volunteers."

The second *C* in Hiltz's approach is Collaboration. This one is especially important to the community organization, which expects transparency and openness from leadership.

"The collaboration piece is something I've built into my career," said Hiltz. "I try to describe my philosophy as servant leadership."

"Look, the good administrators are servant leaders. They work for the clinical staff. They try to make things easier."

"I intend to make this organization a great place to practice medicine, a great place to work, including nursing as a profession, and a great place to be a patient. If we as a team treat each other like family, our patients like we would treat family members, and the organization as our home, then we're going to win."

Collaboration will be at the core of the Hiltz administration, from staff to physicians and donors alike.

The third *C* in the approach is Connection—a characteristic dependent on the previous two.

"I think one of the things that's vitally important in healthcare right now is that notion of being connected to the community because healthcare is a team sport, for sure," said Hiltz. "You can't do everything inside the four walls of a hospital. It must connect to the public health agencies and other community partners. I'll be building on the great connections you already have. Those are some things that I think would be a hallmark of our working together. If we can do that, I think we've got a wildly successful future."

While Hiltz's vision focuses on the C's, one specific C stands out with the institution.

"And when talking about the C's, there's one that's more important—and that's Care," said Hiltz when speaking specifically about NCH. "In the homework I did on what you do here at NCH, the care you deliver is phenomenal. Just speaking with some of you, I know you're passionate about delivering world-class patient care."

"I love your mission here to help people live longer, healthier, happier lives."

We set up interviews with all critical news media, such as TV, radio, and print, with those assigned to the health beat being the first to have the breaking news. We purchased half-page ads in the *Naples Daily News*.

Naples Daily News's Bill Barker recalled they connected quickly when Paul first came to town. He found Paul a breath of fresh air.

"He's astute to know what the job was, to reestablish community trust in the healthcare organization and faith. He knew the media would be an important part of that, an important player."

Barker was appreciative of Paul reaching out to him.

🔧 LEADERSHIP TOOL KIT (PAUL)
SHINING LIGHT

Bill Barker of the *Naples Daily News* commented on the proper attitude regarding the relationship with local news media. He noted that business becomes a microcosm of the community, and the more it reflects that community, the better the business. "That's what all businesses seek. Paul came in with a clarity of understanding that was important. Having been in politics (on Council in Ohio) and under the light of media, I always said, 'you shine light, you find your own way,' a scriptures motto. I love it. We could shine light on things, and he knew the importance of that. He also knew that you must manage that, not in a negative way, but be receptive to it. If you can't, I've told many politicians, CEOs, and others you should never be intimidated by the press. The press is the most valuable training ground you could ever find to overcome objections. What I always wanted as an outcome was that leadership to become sources for my reporting crew, and they would become advocacy for the quality of our media, the quality of the work we do, and the interest we have in common: to genuinely help the community advance itself."

Naples Daily News reporters reacted to the news and interviewed Kevin Beebe, one of ten members of NCH's executive search committee.

During interviews, Beebe said that Hiltz demonstrated he's an innovative and visionary leader with creative ideas. However, NCH's board chose him more for his track record of building a community through collaboration with physicians, administrators, community leaders, and other stakeholders.

Beebe added that he was not surprised to see so many qualified candidates apply.

"It is reinforcement that we have a healthcare system in this community that is well regarded outside of Naples," Beebe noted.[29]

+ + +

The week after the press announcement was hectic, answering dozens of inquiries from journalists around the region, coordinating interviews, and spreading the good news.

A general e-blast focused on the introduction was sent to our entire digital mailing list. A special web page with Paul's information and bio, as well as the NCH website digital banner, went live. Our introduction blog message and social posts from NCH and Paul were sent out.

Shortly after, we shifted our communications to deliver a broader story about Paul. Where the first phase focused on more "bio-type" background information, this next phase focused on revealing more personal aspects of Paul. We lead with vision and philosophy content supported by his background.

We're giving him the ball. Just watch.

—BOARD MEMBER

While September 3, 2019, marked the first official day for Paul Hiltz at NCH, he had previously visited the community. He enjoyed

---

29   Ibid.

clandestinely registering as a hospital visitor, watching and listening as he traveled incognito through the NCH facilities.

Hiltz created a vision for the institution, drawing inspiration from the mission that has made NCH a leader for many years. He also explained the need to strive for relationships with on-staff physicians, the independent physician community, nurses, and technicians—his "pluralistic approach" to administration.

"Build better and better relationships with doctors," said Hiltz. "Let's try to eliminate roadblocks and make it fun for doctors to practice medicine."

"We've done a lot of growing," said former chief human resources officer Renee Thigpen.

Renee Thigpen

"We had an important shift in our culture, where it's not so bureaucratic, and people can make choices and try new things."

She said that the team collaborates and communicates well, and while that was something that previously existed, it did so in silos.

"Not everyone had that full potential or ability to drive things forward. It was a very intensely managed environment. And at the time, that seemed normal," she added.

"Sometimes, you don't know what you don't know until you get out of it and see a different perspective. One of the greatest outcomes was growing and engaging employees in ways we hadn't before."

"It's a nice change from the past, and I'm very encouraged by his openness to collaborating with everyone—nurses, techs, the whole team," said Jonathan Kling, RN, COO.

"I think we, as a team, if we can build these relationships in our community, we're going to have a lot more fun," said Hiltz, "and thereby, we'll do a better job of caring for our community."

With almost forty years of human resources experience, Renee Thigpen has a unique perspective on NCH leadership styles.

She described the previous administration, early on, as highly gracious and well respected by the employees. They rounded frequently. They knew employees by name. They knew what their children did and what sports they played. They just connected, but not as well as Paul does with the community.

Renee recalled that she immediately recognized Paul Hiltz as very collaborative, easygoing, determined to meet goals and guidelines, and has high expectations but very gracious when working with you and setting those expectations.

"Paul just has this air to him about bringing people together. He is very holistic, creating a pluralistic environment where everybody has a voice. Paul has included the providers in communications and decisions and involved them in leadership programs. He created that atmosphere of autonomy to make decisions and offer suggestions without fear of retaliation."

"There's no fear if something happens that didn't go the right way. We look at how we can adjust. How can we pivot? And let's go back at it again. Lots of collaborative communication."

A NEW COVENANT

During Paul's final interview with the search committee, Mariann MacDonald openly expressed concern that perhaps Paul may be a bit too calm. "Maybe so," he responded. "Nothing much shakes me up after four decades of hospital leadership."

His first day of work in Naples was about seven months after the protests and disruption settled.

What has been missing has been a dedicated effort to create a sense of belonging.

LEADERSHIP TOOL KIT (PAUL)
LISTENING TOUR

A new leader should prioritize visiting all the stakeholders as much as possible and demonstrate sincere listening. These folks needed that, and the impact was apparent from the outset. People want that visit. Civic groups want that visit. They want to know that they matter. We devoted the first ninety days to meeting the community leaders and listening to the physicians, hospital supporters, and employees. The work of a health system went on while we showed the flag. What many called a fresh, welcome leadership style helped bring the Naples and Collier County community closer together. From weekly briefings to town halls, we beckoned the community back, facing skeptics with openness and sincerity, offering a sense of belonging and partnership.

This new team reached out as if asking for a new covenant, a request of everyone in Naples to take a closer look at what their *community healthcare* means to them. We honored the devotion of founders, physicians, nurses, employees, and those who raised funds and volunteered their time to improve NCH.

"We could never find a better listener anywhere," a longtime employee said.

Paul recalled some wisdom from a powerful mentor, David Jimenez, a senior partner in the CEO Advisory Network, who has been named one of the *Top 100 Most Powerful People in Healthcare*. David specializes in clinical transformation problems.

"David told me that communication is the central thing in a turnaround. It's not finance. It's not human resources. You must keep the people with you. You've got to tell them everything that is happening," Paul recalled.

One of our priorities after the opening events was to speak to NCH volunteers as a group. We posted Paul's message on the NCH website.

"I always tell volunteers that you do as much to uplift the employees' spirits as anything I know. You are smiling, and you're there, and employees are appreciative. Just to see a friendly face that doesn't want anything and isn't going to yell at you for anything … that's invaluable support for our team."

⚒ LEADERSHIP TOOL KIT (PAUL)
CAN YOU GUESS MY NAME?

We spent a large part of each day making rounds, speaking to the staff, and asking if they had everything they needed. People who rounded with us noted that the leadership team has an amazing memory for names and faces, and walking the halls with us taught us a lesson in that skill. We will probably recall your name immediately if we have ever met you. It was essential to us, a crucial part of reengaging the staff, and a skill set that can be learned.

We shaped and lived our new mission: *to help people live longer, healthier, happier lives.* We began to get out into organizations and schools and educate people on this.

Twenty years ago, it was normal for us in healthcare to do something (long pause) and then (perhaps) tell people about it.

At NCH, something different began to occur. We formed a team. Once we got into a rhythm of working together closely, decisions were made in collaboration. All the public relations and branding considerations were considered at the time of operational decision-making.

Communications became the heart of the turnaround. There is no longer a wall between operational decisions and communications. It's gone. The Partnership's relationship with the administration included selecting team leaders. The people are part of the brand.

But then from the agency perspective, the world has changed as well. The agency model (it's not the "Mad Men" as depicted on the TV series of that name) has evolved and today you truly must roll up your sleeves and be a partner with your clients. Our partnership approach to problem-solving, and providing strategic solutions and recommendations, requires complete immersion in the business.

In late October 2019, we dealt with a negative news report in the *Naples Daily News* regarding our D Grade from the Leapfrog organization. The Leapfrog Hospital Survey performs an annual voluntary survey in which they ask hospitals to report quality and safety data and then publicly reports that information, by hospital. Most data used to calculate the Safety Grade comes from the Centers for Medicare & Medicaid Services.

Following our transparency promise, we willingly provided the news media with the same information received by our board.

"While this would never be acceptable for any organization, it is not accurate. Allow me to offer context," Paul explained.

NCH decided not to participate in the Leapfrog survey in the spring of 2019. This was during the interim CEO period, and leadership decided not to participate in the survey. Failing to participate in the survey meant that the Leapfrog organization had to use historical data, sometimes as far back as five years old, to reach their finding.

Given the circumstances, Leapfrog graded NCH a D instead of an "incomplete."

"NCH has typically participated in Leapfrog surveys in the past; however, declining to participate is not unusual. In fact, 30 percent of organizations choose not to participate in the survey for many reasons," he added.

🔧 PR TOOL KIT (AMANDA)
SOLID MEDIA RELATIONS

The goal of solid media relations is fairness. Throughout the upheaval, reporters at the Naples media have been pleased at the total access we gave them, responding to inquiries immediately. While we may get negative press coverage from time to time it usually has been fair, and we always respond before publication or airing. In addition, our credibility has been enhanced with reporters, who are important players in the community, and colleagues who help shape reputations. But once you willingly demonstrate transparency, there is more opportunity for negative press to occur. That means the initiative is unfolding as it should. In the long term, the news media will approach us with a greater sense of fairness and be a resource for information to our community.

Naples Daily News's Bill Barker noted that "the reason that Paul and I were able to appreciate what each other was trying to do, was his appreciation for the hard job that media has been trying to do, particularly today. Yet I understood, and still believe wholeheartedly, that our number one mission is to strengthen this community. We cannot be a strong community without a strong healthcare organization."

Jim Mahon, PhD, who had been a colleague of Paul Hiltz's for years, joined NCH about two months after Paul arrived and took over as senior vice president of philanthropy. He joined Paul for numerous community gatherings.

"We had a lot of *meet-and-greets,* and we were doing a lot of *cleanup on aisle six,* and reestablishing relationships with other community organizations. About a dozen folks hosted the events for us," Dr. Mahon recalled.

A great example of that can be seen in Paul's ninety-day progress report we offered the *Naples Daily News*. The newspaper printed it verbatim.

December 5, 2019

My 90-Day Listening Tour

by Paul Hiltz for the Naples Daily News[30]

When I arrived in Naples over Labor Day weekend, I first called our chief nursing officer, Jon Kling, RN, to schedule a night round at NCH. The reason for this was twofold. First, the night crew seldom gets the recognition it deserves, and I wanted to introduce myself personally to show how important solidarity is to me. The second was to begin my ninety-day listening tour.

Listening tours are instrumental during onboarding when you're new to an organization. Just like learning about the process and where to park, connecting with your staff, who are key to any successful organization, should be a priority.

I made it a point to connect with physicians, nurses, administrators, and staff so that I could better learn about NCH from the people that serve this community so well.

One big takeaway was making this a community hospital where all physicians are welcome. My response was this: We are, and should always be, a community hospital—it's in our name.

---

30   Liz Freeman, "Chief Executive Officer of NCH Paul Hiltz Looks Back at First 90 Days," *Naples Daily News*, January 10, 2020, accessed November 15, 2021, https://www.naplesnews.com/story/news/health/2020/01/10/chief-executive-officer-of-nch-paul-hiltz-looks-back-at-first-90-days/4431761002/.

I'm proud to share that we recently received some amazing accolades. First, we earned the coveted four stars from CMS, which everyone's excited about. We were named in the top 250 hospitals nationally by Healthgrades, a respected scoring system. And, of course, we were recognized by *U.S. News & World Report* as a best regional hospital—specifically in six types of care—which is a big deal for NCH.

All these awards speak to our dedication to our mission to help our community live happier, healthier lives.

NCH is also widely recognized for our quality care, specifically when it comes to emergency care and stroke care.

We are committed to maintaining a high level of excellence and our donors play a large role in our success. Their contributions are what make NCH a leader in Southwest Florida.

Outside the walls of our healthcare system is another great advantage to living and working in Naples, the community. Both my wife Kris and I were blessed with a warm welcome the moment we arrived. Since then, we've met with hundreds of folks in the community, and we've quickly realized that they want our community healthcare system to be as successful as we do. In fact, when you have the power of community behind you, there's nothing you can't accomplish.

I'm proud to say that my first ninety days on the job have been met with open arms by the community, collaboration with physicians and staff, connections with the entire NCH family, and most importantly a dedication to patient care.

Ninety days later, I am even more excited about the future of our organization. The passion and the commitment to patient care that is universally shared by our NCH family is inspiring. But I'm not done listening. While the official tour is over, I look forward to continued conversations and collaboration. Listening is an important part of my leadership style and I continue to learn about how we can continue to build on the excellence at NCH.

Thanks for your warm welcome to this community. We are looking forward to our health future, together.

Welcome to Florida, Paul. Here's a hurricane.

Jonathan Kling, RN, NCH chief nursing officer, recalled the night he took Paul on that tour of the evening and night shifts.

"I remember that because he flew down, and we had a hurricane spinning off the coast, and I wondered if his flight would make it in. In the middle of the night, we went to the floors. I remember thinking, *Wow, here is a leader in healthcare who is not a physician or a clinician, who still understood the language of healthcare.* He was so personable that people just wanted to talk to him. I remember thinking, *Wow, this is the genesis of a new day.* Because if we can talk and work together on problems, we're good. But man, good to great could be achievable here. For me, that was kind of my *aha* moment in the middle of the night with Paul."

Jonathan Kling, RN

"He was a different CEO. He said, 'Jon, you're a clinician. We want to be a clinically driven organization and have our clinical leaders and doctors and nurses making decisions in a collaborative, pluralistic manner.'"

As a clinician, nurse, and patient advocate, that was music to my ears.

+ + +

Meanwhile, we carefully began to rebuild the NCH management. We saw casualties from the changes as we examined the executive team closely, especially regarding employee morale. We needed solid managers willing to leave it all on the field, listen to their employees, and challenge negativity.

🔧 LEADERSHIP TOOL KIT (PAUL)
MOVING ON UP

We explain to younger people entering management that you should not come into an organization thinking you will gradually move up the leadership scale. Your job as a leader is to go in and solve a problem. And if you solve it, the good news is you will get a bigger problem to solve next time. And that's how you move up in an organization. And the people that we've recruited and attracted are people that like to solve problems. They don't shy away from it.

**Today, a brand is no longer just a slogan.
It's what you do.**

We were reminded of the wording for the CEO opportunity at NCH, as published by the search firm Russell Reynolds: "[T] he new president and CEO will have the opportunity to establish a legacy by advancing the healthcare system during a time of critical transformation."

What does the organization mean to the community? What is the exchange relationship? What is the promise? What is the connection? Is there a covenant? Today, a brand is no longer just a slogan. It's what you do.

Healthcare has changed dramatically in the last decade. Leaders who have picked up on that are ready for their career to meet the future. It was easy to see why the art of listening, the ability to project a likable light touch, can open a new door to transparency and openness and, ultimately, to mutual confidence and understanding.

Career journalist Bill Barker said it best.

Paul spent some time in public life, he said. "He understood public sentiment, right? He knew the public can be persnickety and fickle and that you must understand that there are a lot of diverse opinions. He valued the importance of open and honest transparency in communications."

Our listening tour was especially intense internally. We listened to the people throughout the organization. We wanted to know what they thought and what they would do. Our administrative team shadowed physicians to "walk a mile in their shoes" to hear what's on their minds. We also tasked all managers to visit their operations on all shifts regularly. Some people call that "management by walking around." We call it leadership.

Paul summed it up at a management meeting.

"The basic way we are handling this is we are just trying to get people to think slightly differently here. And then we'll all move together to get to the right destination."

We envisioned growing the orthopedic surgery, general surgery, and cardiology programs. We wanted more primary care doctors. This is such a vital part of medicine that there are never enough. When there is a shortage or practices are not accessible enough, people go to the emergency room unnecessarily. We had a lot of work to do internally. We wanted employees to feel free to speak up, let us know what they need, and feel a sense of belonging.

🛠 BRANDING TOOL KIT (AMANDA)
THE MODERN DESIRE TO BELONG

When rebuilding a brand identity, we encourage creating a sense of belonging, leaning into the moments that matter most between brand and consumer.

We seek to connect the brand and the consumer in every way we can.

We love research that helps us uncover powerful human insights. This involves crafting measurable, meaningful, and compelling creative communication. The modern desire to belong has evolved in today's digitally connected world. It takes something special to create a true sense of brand belonging. It starts with a strategic purpose, is defined through a deep understanding of social science, grows from creative solutions, and flourishes with well-crafted execution. Building brands this way works.

A sense of belonging between business and consumer is no longer a luxury. It's a necessity. The average consumer is exposed to ten thousand brand messages a day, attention spans have dropped from twelve to eight seconds over the last fifteen years, and audiences switch between screens up to twenty-one times an hour.

Belonging is also good business.

- Top brands that create belonging grew revenue over six years at three times the rate of lower-performing brands.
- Top brands that create belonging gained market share up to 10 percent over three years.

- Top brands that create belonging have an 8 percent higher rate in purchase-funnel conversion.
- Top brands that create belonging are 9 percent more likely to be recommended than lower-performing brands.

We started a series of forums for employees to articulate issues. It was slow initially, but soon, our team began to see that we intended to improve things, and folks became more vocal.

Shortly after Paul's arrival, we took a big step toward improving the relationship with Lee Health by selling NCH equity in the Bonita Community Health Center, a joint operation with Lee Health since 2000, when relations were more cordial. The Bonita Center for outpatient services had incurred considerable debt, yet we were battling this out in court over severing ties and resolving management disputes. We now quickly agreed to fair terms, and the two hospital organizations entered a new era of collaboration.

In a joint press release, Dr. Larry Antonucci, CEO of Lee Health, concurred.

"We have a strong relationship with NCH, and it has been a pleasure to work with Paul on collaborative opportunities to improve care in our region," Dr. Antonucci said in a statement. "As the two largest healthcare providers in Southwest Florida, a closer relationship between Lee Health and NCH benefits our community and the patients we serve."

HAVING A BALL

An extensive expansion of the NCH Downtown Baker Hospital emergency room, pegged to cost $35 million, got underway, which was the recipient of proceeds from the Ball on November 9, 2019.

That event, a welcome celebration, was a sigh of relief by the healthcare family. It was over. This was a new day. We received the biggest ovation when we announced that NCH would seek a *Top 100 Hospital* honor by Healthgrades. It was a declaration. A successful event by any measure, we raised about $2.1 million of the ER expansion cost at the 2019 NCH Ball. The faithful were coming back. But equally important, there was a mood shift that night. The whole celebration was exuberant. Our hospital family had a great time: live music, dancing, great food, and conversation.[31]

BRANDING TOOL KIT (AMANDA)
PARTNERSHIP OVER PRESENTATION™

As we sought a new partnership between the community and the healthcare system, our agency was simultaneously building a true partnership with the board and Paul Hiltz. Belonging can't happen without partnership. This philosophy reveals the strength in true client/agency teams, that working sessions are more productive than meetings, and that partnership is far more valuable than presentation.

The *Naples Daily News* published an article after Paul Hiltz's first ninety days here, reporting that Paul noted his "top priorities are emphasizing that NCH is a community hospital where independent physicians and employed physicians can work side by side; improving the patient culture; and focusing on quality."

---

31   NCH, "2019 NCH Hospital Ball Recap," YouTube, December 16, 2019, accessed September 1, 2021, https://www.youtube.com/watch?v=8K8LNOQoHs0.

The brand reputation has a direct impact to the bottom line and was a hit on our operating income, which was $39 million in 2018, while 2019 went south to a loss of $2.9 million. That's not a catastrophe on a $656 million revenue picture, but it illustrated the damage when an organization goes through this kind of disruption.

Dr. Jim Mahon, who worked with Paul in his previous endeavors, has watched him create excellence for thirty years.

"Paul cut his professional teeth on the physician side. He ran physician groups and spent many years just working purely in the doctors' world. And that's why he is such a great fit because that's where his heart is; it's with having these administrative dyads where you have an administrator and a physician at the same level working together. Paul comes by this very naturally through his career."

Our listening tour seemed to have impact. We began to reestablish relationships with the Chamber of Commerce, and with the county, with the city, and other key healthcare organizations.

PR TOOL KIT (AMANDA)
TIMING

This community needed to feel comfortable with the way we fulfill our mission before we launch new communications with new brand promises. People must begin to see and feel the change we were promising. Our brand promise was the mantra of our mission. That's enough at this point in the journey, when added to a flow of positive news coming from NCH.

NCH created the new position of chief quality officer to analyze outcomes and to create NCH's own quality scores. The organization had never established the role of quality officer. Dr. Carlos Quintero was promoted to our team.

Dr. Quintero has been with NCH since 2006. He recalls his first days as chief quality officer.

"When I took the role of acute quality officer, I was still seeing patients about 75 percent of the time. So I had a unique look or perspective, should I say, because I was still seeing patients at the bedside just like all the other physicians were, and at the same time trying to build a larger team to address quality issues in the system."

"I didn't know it at the time, but the stress and frustration of living through the community disruption and opposition to our hospitalist pilot program prepared me for the coming crises," where the very presence of hospitalists staffing our hospitals instantly became a life-and-death matter, Dr. Quintero recalled.

A big quality project was already in motion. Plans were launched to convert all semiprivate rooms at both hospitals to private rooms, which was way overdue, and a big plus for everyone.

It was now time to rebuild and mend fences. In fact, we tried to rip down those fences, with prejudice. We visited the clinic, and immediately encouraged them to send patients again to NCH. We encouraged employees and doctors to volunteer there. We renewed our sponsorships with them. We were gratified that cofounder Nancy Lascheid told the newspaper that the relationship with us was now positive.[32]

"His perspective regarding the importance of community collaboration is reassuring," Lascheid said. "The relationship between NCH and the Neighborhood Health Clinic continues forward in fulfilling the scope of medical care. We welcome Paul Hiltz and his leadership."

We renewed relationships with the Healthcare Network of Southwest Florida, which operates outpatient offices throughout

---

32   Freeman, "Chief Executive Officer of NCH Paul Hiltz Looks Back at First 90 Days."

Collier, and fulfills an important role, said Emily Ptaszek, chief executive officer of Healthcare Network.

"I very much trust his transparency and that there will be a much closer collaboration than we have seen historically," Emily Ptaszek said to the *Naples Daily News*.[33]

We also cleared the air with competitor Scott Lowe, the CEO of nearby Physicians Regional Healthcare, and we all hoped for a new day of working together.

🛠 LEADERSHIP TOOL KIT (PAUL)
PLURALISM AND POWER

We were living in the transition to a more pluralistic model of organization. Here was a community demanding collaboration, partnerships, involvement, and listening. In the past, this may have been lip service. Now, it needed to happen. This new paradigm, pluralism, can be defined as a social construct where multiple people, groups, or entities share political power or influence. In our story thus far, consider who needed a say in NCH's future: city and county elected officials, physicians, employees, volunteers, vocal citizens, civic groups, associations, former leadership, patients, and donors.

The *Naples Daily News* reported that Mayor Bill Barnett said that Hiltz has made himself visible in the community. "I'm getting good feedback," Barnett said.

"He's approachable. That goes a long way."

---

33   Ibid.

"It is getting there," Barnett said.

When a new CEO comes into an organization, it's bad form to step in and start making wholesale changes in the leadership. While we may decide that some folks are in the wrong role, changes should be done carefully. We eliminated some vacant positions and created new ones along the way. About a year after The Partnership arrived in Naples, NCH restructured several leadership positions in public relations and communications. This is when Amanda Lucey assumed a leadership role while continuing to lead the agency's full creative power. We shuffled physician liaison responsibilities and strategy and business development roles. We wanted someone waking up every morning thinking about how to grow the business.

The press release explained this unique and progressive partnership.

"Lucey brings a talented team of creatives, account leaders, digital experts, and developers to support every aspect of the NCH marketing and PR strategy. Recently, Lucey had been recognized for building the fastest-growing female-owned brand communications agency in the Southeast. She prides herself on developing purpose-driven partnerships including her work with Children's Healthcare of Atlanta, the British Embassy, the Department of Agriculture, and the International Continental Hotel Group."

One of the reasons that we have not been in a rush to change the identity and brand of NCH was that we were in the middle of some big changes, a major listening tour, building a new NCH Heart Institute, talking about partnering with a national group for outpatient care, moving toward reconfiguring our orthopedic services, and building service lines.

+ + +

AN OVERALL TURNAROUND STRATEGY

As we settled into our new roles, Paul explained to the leadership team that his background of success is based on partnerships not only with the community and the staff of the organization but with the best and brightest organizations in America's healthcare.

If you don't define yourself, someone else will ...

We had both entered an organization needing a turnaround strategy. We noted that Amanda's key to successful client relationships has always been a partnership philosophy, creating belonging in every agency relationship. This was not to be improvisational. We quickly agreed that our efforts would be deliberate and strategic.

Do we lead NCH back to the old ways of thinking? Or do we cut our teeth on being willing to transform and becoming agile?

Paul brought along his Rolodex filled with contacts at some of the top consultancies in the country. So, just as we initially reached out to every community leader we could get in front of and every physician, employee, volunteer, and retiree we could gather, we began implementing what we internally dubbed the Turnaround Game Plan.

NCH is at an inflection point. The right strategic moves at the right time can set the foundation for a different future, which is what the board of trustees wants. It's what the physicians want. After the upheaval of the past year, we can only hope the employees, volunteers, and donors can aspire to that as well.

We would start by working on the culture and the relationships and educating people about the situation here and explaining to everybody that we can exactly know how the business model works and how we get paid. Things move a little faster once people understand the organization's condition and how people can help take the waste out of an organization. That formed step one, with intense emphasis on the physicians. We had a lot of communicating to do and a lot of trust to build.

The one thing we heard clearly from the outset is that the people of Southwest Florida will not settle for anything but the best healthcare available, so our efforts intensified to attract some of America's top doctors in several specialties. At this time, a movement had already begun to create true centers of excellence around several specialties, such as our cancer center, heart institute, orthopedics, women's health, and physical rehabilitation. Already a core partner with the Mayo Clinic, we also sought to tighten ties with the Cleveland Clinic.

Paul's career has always been about creating "best practices," not trying to reinvent healthcare but bringing in people who understand the nation's (ever-changing) best practices to help guide our company. We knew the medical records system needed complete reinvention, so we began a multiyear partnership with Epic to provide us with the best integrated medical records system available.

Within that new world order, we would be looking at labor management, and we would seek to create a partnership with a brilliant company called Capital Consulting that helped us teach managers and directors how to manage their labor and flex it up and down with volumes.

Not long after that, we would focus on our revenue cycle and make sure that our bills are accurate, timely, and efficient. So we began to examine partnering with one of the nation's most respected consultancies, Ensemble.

The advancement of quality included a strategic partnership with ProScan, a national leader in imaging. If we are to attract the best and brightest physicians, our clinical imaging must be second to none.

With Florida's older retiring population, our clinical leaders often list advancement in orthopedics and rehabilitation as top priorities. We began discussions with HSS, the Hospital for Special Surgery in New York, acclaimed as among the best in America.

A firm called Encompass had perfected the art of running successful physical rehabilitation inpatient facilities, an art form in this day and age, so we looked to a partnership with these healthcare specialists.

So we built our playbook, our strategic imperative. *Lead, follow, or get out of the way.*

In mental health, the market leader was not NCH, so instead of competing, we became partners with the market leader, David Lawrence Centers.

We did the same with neonatal intensive care. NCH collaborates with the world-renowned Nicklaus Children's Health System, the parent organization of Nicklaus Children's Hospital, to provide care in the neonatal intensive care unit (NICU).

In summary, our strategy was to continuously improve the quality of every aspect of the NCH brand of healthcare. Every day. Fix the culture. Chase the best quality care every day. That will lead us to robust financial performance.

New Partnerships to Transform Excellence
HSS (Hospital for Special Surgery)

HSS at NCH will design and build the most advanced medical facility at the North Naples Hospital campus. That facility will be more than eighty thousand square feet and a destination for comprehensive outpatient and inpatient musculoskeletal services, including a jointly owned and operated ambulatory surgery center, clinics, imaging, and rehabilitation services. The pioneering collaboration is part of NCH's transformation to become an Advanced Community Healthcare System™.

#1 in Orthopedics by U.S. News & World Report fourteen years in a row

#2 in Rheumatology by U.S. News & World Report[34]

Epic

Empowering over 185 million patients to get and stay healthy, Epic is famously known as one of the first electronic health record (EHR) providers and supports some of the world's biggest healthcare systems. Since its founding in 1979, Epic's long-standing reputation and experience boasts easy scalability and effective products and services.[35]

Ensemble Health Partners

A tech-driven end-to-end revenue cycle outsourcing firm that helps healthcare providers focus on what matters most, with staggering client loyalty across the nation.[36]

Encompass Health

As a leading provider of inpatient rehabilitation for stroke, brain injury, hip fracture, and other complex neurological and orthopedic conditions, we meet patients where they are in their recovery. When choosing Encompass Health for rehabilitation, our patients

---

34   HHS, Hospital for Special Surgery, accessed January 22, 2024, https://www.hss.edu/.

35   Epic, accessed January 22, 2024, https://www.epic.com/.

36   Ensemble Health Partners, accessed January 22, 2024, https://www.ensemblehp.com/.

receive compassionate care from an expert team of physical, occupational, and speech therapists, physicians, nurses, dietitians, pharmacists, and case managers who work together to create a plan to help meet their unique goals.[37]

ProScan® Clinical Imaging

ProScan® Imaging is one of the largest outpatient imaging networks in the country, with thirty-three centers in five regions, including Ohio, Indiana, Kentucky, New York, and Florida. They provide high-quality diagnostic imaging at affordable prices in convenient, comfortable surroundings.

C2 Healthcare
Capital Consulting Labor Management

C2 Healthcare combines the business intelligence of the OPTIX (a cost-based labor management system) reporting system with proven coaching models, elevating your operational efficiency and effectiveness by realizing unmatched labor savings and fostering a culture of continuous improvement.[38]

And then there were rumors of a pandemic. Looming on the horizon, beyond the clear vision of most of us in American healthcare, lurked the greatest public health disaster in our lifetime. As time passed and more and more news came out about it, it felt like an approaching hurricane. We would not know how bad it was going

---

37   Encompass Rehab Health, accessed January 22, 2024, https://encompasshealth.com/.

38   The C2 Difference, accessed January 22, 2024, https://c2healthcare.com.

to get until it got very close. The full humanity of our role rapidly became apparent.

From a branding perspective, our months of listening and learning were beginning to pay off. Remembering the age-old tenet that if you don't define yourself, someone else will, we discussed reshaping the health system's brand identity. Many experts would suggest that a change of identity could be considered. But our intuition was that now was not the time for that. We needed to hold onto the history, heritage, and deep community ties at NCH with every ounce of strength we had. In addition, deep and steady collaboration would take more time. A new branding campaign cannot be developed in a closed room and revealed as a fait accompli.

The brand began to shift even before the pandemic arrived in Naples. As we were enjoying the final weeks of our listening tour, doing our road show, the subject matter changed. People wanted to know what we knew about the virus. We began to share everything we knew with the community. We streamlined full access by the news media to our doctors. We quickly saw the need for a continuous flow of information accessible to everyone in Collier County and Naples, and beyond.

Our early work in the community set the stage to be able to make things happen. Our listening tour had rolled on for almost five months, yet that was not nearly enough time to fully restore all the negativity and all the relationships that were broken, or that didn't even exist in the community. And of course, being new, we were just establishing relationships. Now we had to prepare for a major public health disaster.

Dr. Jim Mahon noted that when January arrived, it became obvious that Paul was a great leader.

"He saw this ahead of most CEOs and by January, we had a COVID task force led by Dr. David Linder meeting every day. We had daily conversations with our colleagues at Mayo Clinic. We made sure our supply chain was good with personal protective equipment (PPE). Paul was ahead. He knows his stuff."

On January 21, 2020, the Centers for Disease Control and Protection confirmed the first US coronavirus case. Ten days later, the World Health Organization (WHO) issued a Global Health Emergency, the sixth such alert in history. Human-to-human transmission quickly spread and was found in the United States, Germany, Japan, Vietnam, and Taiwan.

On February 3, the United States declared a Public Health Emergency. This news made it clear that NCH may have to activate the pandemic plan that has been established.

In late February, we announced we had over sixty isolation rooms in the system. These rooms look almost like any other patient room, but airflow circulates to be removed through ductwork with a HEPA filter in place, thus providing safe discharge of any airborne particles.

Interim chief medical officer Dr. Bryan Murphey recalled they had very little to go on then. After all, the United States is not acquainted with pandemics, the last widespread pandemic was the flu epidemic of 1918.

Specifically, NCH had been closely monitoring the novel coronavirus since it first appeared in the media and through patient care studies published in the medical journals *Lancet* and *JAMA* in February. This was the start of the crisis. We just didn't know it yet. They were calling it the "novel coronavirus" at first. By March, it was called COVID-19. In Florida, things began to unfold quickly. On March 5, 2020, Lee Health in Ft. Myers reported its first COVID-19 patient death, representing the first recorded virus-related fatality in Florida. As we were visiting the Downtown Baker facility on March 7 to make rounds and visit with patients, everything blew up. We got an alert on our cell phones.

"It's here."

Renee Thigpen was on call when the first COVID-19 patient arrived. It was a Sunday. She came into the administration office. Chief nursing officer Jon Kling was there.

"We set up a base to start fielding calls, working on policies, getting supplies in, developing incentive plans, and deciding how and where to test patients."

"The first thing we knew was we needed supplies. A lot of supplies," Dr. Murphey recalled.

"We reached out to colleagues across the country and the world. What is the best practice to take care of a patient? How can we protect our staff, respiratory therapists, nurses, critical care physicians, pulmonary physicians, and patients? This was before any vaccines or treatment protocols, or medications came along."

"It's interesting to recall a husband and wife visiting our office in early January. These patients were in Wuhan, China, in late November 2019. They got sick. They came back to Naples with cough and cold symptoms. To this day, we don't know if they had COVID-19. We now know that antibodies only last about six months, so we are uncertain if it was that or another respiratory infection," Dr. Murphey said.

Dr. Murphey noted that we didn't get the testing ability until the early summer of 2020, so there was no way to tell for sure back then.

There was already a lot of controversy about masking among Floridians.

"We all know that masks work because gas masks work," Dr. Murphey noted, alluding to the military usage.

"It comes down to what type of mask a person has and how it fits to their face. So the two things least discussed are: what type and how it fits. You can have an N95 mask with a large gap around the nose, so it may not work. If it's hard to breathe through, then you have a chance that it is working. And in humid south Florida, nobody wants to wear a sweaty mask on their face."

How to Build Teams in a Crisis
Jonathan Kling, RN, NCH chief nursing officer, and cochair, COVID-19 Task Force

We learned a lot as we stepped up to prepare for the attack of COVID-19 in Naples and Collier County.

I think it's important to have a "charter statement."

What is the goal of this team?

Try to anticipate what will happen from operations, knowledge of colleagues around the nation, and expertise. What's going to be necessary?

I was blessed from the first day I was appointed to the task force that several folks like Dr. David Lindner approached me to say, "Can I be part of this?" I didn't have to market it too hard.

I said, "Coming into this team, there are no titles. You may be the medical director, and I may be the executive sponsor of this team, but we make decisions together. We rise and fall together. Could you support that?" He agreed.

This was more than just an NCH problem. This was a community problem. We needed to collaborate and reach out to folks that we seldom worked with in the past, such as competing healthcare systems here in our market, not-for-profit agencies in health-care, and the Collier County Public Schools. We added a daily call with everybody and said, what are you doing?

We all needed to know that there would be times when we were going to make decisions that were not popular. Still, if our focus were to make it as safe and compassionate as possible, if that were our mission and we stayed to it, then we'd be successful.

At maturity, our COVID-19 Task Force was ten people internally. Our entire team was close to one hundred, which was beautiful because that included Lee Health, Physicians Regional Medical Center, Healthcare Network of Southwest Florida, Neighborhood Health Clinic, the Department of Health for Collier County, and Collier County Public Schools. They were coming out of the woodwork to want to work together. It was wonderful. Seven days a week, every day from March 2020 to November 2021, we gathered for that fifteen- to thirty-minute call, eighteen months straight.

That kept me going in those dark days when I was getting four hours of sleep and getting yelled at for making folks wear masks. The dedication to our community and our patients and staff through all this was the rewarding part for me. That's what kept a person like me going. My wife was wonderful. She supported me so much. She's a nurse practitioner at her hospital, so she took a leave to take care of our kids because there was no school, and I was not home. I would not be here without her.

For months, our team spoke several times a day. Communication was key to letting our board members, community, and staff know exactly what was happening. And that notion has been the theme for the success of our entire story. Communication.

When we gathered the team, we looked for expertise. We needed an infectious disease doctor who was passionate about research. We needed physicians who knew what their frontline workers faced and could be that voice to the doctors. We made sure that our supply chain leader knew that he or she would make decisions without being micromanaged.

The structure of setting it up becomes more important than the people. Culture rules. If you don't set up the right mindset, you could have the best people and not succeed.

"There was enormous fear and uncertainty," Dr. Quintero recalled.

"But setting that aside, there was also a very great sense of comradery in that this is our job and our calling to take care of these patients and to do whatever we needed to do and put whatever we needed to put in place to ensure that we have the teams to take care of the patients," he added.

A tidal wave of patients

"I was also the medical director of the hospitalists simultaneously. So I had a lot of different hats. We put some plans in place and worked very closely with the medical staff leadership to ensure that we had teams in place to take care of what we thought would be a tidal wave of patients we could not handle. So we worked very closely with physicians from different specialties to put teams in place in case our system was bursting at the seams with COVID-19 patients."

It was a tense time, he recalled.

"We didn't know what we would face whenever that tidal wave of patients came. From a quality perspective, the focus was on saving lives. So, we were trying to build a team and stay focused on our big priorities: saving lives, taking care of our employees and clinical staff, and planning so that the staff was safe and had what they needed."

PART 3

THE DARK
VISITOR
ARRIVES

CHAPTER 4

ALL HEROES WEAR MASKS

At first, for weeks, people were not yet wearing masks. Flying back home to Atlanta, Amanda was the only passenger on an evening flight.

"The flight attendant sat down next to me. She was falling apart. The world's going to collapse. They were canceling flights, and everyone was panicking.

"I couldn't blame her," Amanda said, "I was on the edge myself, but in crisis communications, the first rule is to stay calm and smile."

The current COVID-19 pandemic arose in the Wuhan region of China at the end of 2019. By January 2020, China took unprecedented lockdown measures affecting almost a billion people. That did not contain the virus. COVID-19 would affect the world.

The arrival of the COVID-19 pandemic to Europe and North America by February 2020 was followed by lockdowns across the Western world, with varying degrees of restrictions achieving different degrees of success in reigning in the virus. It quickly became apparent that the world would certainly need an immunization program. But the outlook remained bleak as the absolute fastest vaccine that had ever been developed, the mumps vaccine in 1967, was four years in development.[39]

⚒ LEADERSHIP TOOL KIT (PAUL)
GRACE UNDER PRESSURE

We often recall an age-old saying for leaders: "Never let them see you sweat." As Douglas R. Satterfield said in an article appearing in "the Leader Maker," a blog about senior executive leadership, "a leader that can remain levelheaded and calm when the pressure gets turned up, appears highly respected and desirable." "Never let them see you sweat" captures this sentiment well.[40]

Florida was not the first state to reach crisis, so we could collaborate with colleagues in different states about best practices from their viewpoint. There was no guidebook here. We wrote it as we lived through it. In February 2020, we activated our third Xenex Germ-Zapping robot, which was contributed by our board of trustees chair Mariann MacDonald, who was already one of our most loyal donors. These fascinating machines use pulsed, high-intensity, broad-spectrum UV light technology, uniquely lethal to microorganisms, with 99.99 percent of SARS-CoV-2 deactivated in the environment. Disinfection

---

39 Will Brothers, "A Timeline of COVID-19 Vaccine Development," Biospace, December 3, 2020, accessed November 15, 2021, https://www.biospace.com/article/a-timeline-of-covid-19-vaccine-development/.

40 Douglas R. Satterfield, "Never Let Them See You Sweat," Leader Maker, October 29, 2018, accessed November 15, 2021, https://www.theleadermaker.com/never-let-them-see-you-sweat.

cycles are fast, allowing hospitals to disinfect a patient room in as little as ten minutes and surgical suite in twenty minutes or less.

Xenex Disinfection Services is a Texas company that says its robots can kill the scariest pathogens, such as Ebola and anthrax, and the more common germs, such as methicillin-resistant Staphylococcus aureus (MRSA), norovirus, Clostridium difficile, and the flu. The system works on bacteria, viruses, mold, fungi, and spores, according to company officials.

The robots work in five-minute cycles with the pulsed light targeted to disinfect surfaces where germs linger.

"Anything that's close to the patient that is touched frequently, like blood pressure machines, bathrooms, sinks, and doorknobs," said Dr. Vakhtang Bochorishvili, with NCH's Infectious Diseases Department.

NCH is using the robots initially in high-risk areas, such as in ICUs, critical care, operating rooms, emergency departments, and patient rooms, he said.

The WHO declared COVID-19 a pandemic. Tedros Adhanom Ghebreyesus, director general of WHO, said at a briefing in Geneva that the agency was "deeply concerned by the alarming levels of spread and severity" of the outbreak. He also expressed concern about "the alarming levels of inaction."[41]

We entered lockdown. Everybody was in quarantine, and friends around the country were sharing first-person accounts of what was happening with the surging pandemic on the West Coast, how the hospitals responded, and what measures they took.

---

41   Associated Press, "The World Health Organization Declares COVID-19 Outbreak a Pandemic; US Death Toll 31," March 11, 2020, accessed March 13, 2024, https://www.cbs42.com/news/health/coronavirus/8-new-coronavirus-cases-in-florida-cruise-passengers-arrive-in-georgia-for-quarantine/.

Matt Heinle, who would join us in the spring to lead legal affairs, had already been relaying details on what was going on in Ohio and what he was seeing with other healthcare systems. We rebuilt an entire executive team, while rebuilding our reputation, in the middle of this tragic event.

⚒ LEADERSHIP TOOL KIT (PAUL)
COMMAND CENTER

When it became clear this was going to turn into a pandemic, we activated our modified Command Center, creating a new management structure like the disaster planning we always do when a hurricane threatens. We populated the Command Center with clinical leadership, those closest to the action, and enabled them to be the decision-makers, going directly from "need" to "action."

Obviously, we continued with the normal formal structure in place for the other issues like planning a new medical record system, business systems, and general day-to-day decision-making. But in terms of COVID-19, Command Center began making those decisions without going through the normal process to get it done. This sped up everything. Thus, our "COVID-19 Task Force," as we eventually called it, could get emergency credentials for retired physicians and nurses if needed and made all the decisions about masks, visiting hours, shifting staff roles, hiring traveling nurses, and essentially anything to do with clinical needs and patient safety.

Jonathan Kling, RN, recalled what Paul told him when the task force was formed.

"Paul said, 'We're going to let you manage this the way it's supposed to be managed, and we (administration) won't get in the way.'"

"We were hemorrhaging cash, spending money on supplies and equipment and changes to our infrastructure. He didn't step in, and our board supported it. We did a lot of healing because of what we did to support our community and within our organization. We came out of that first wave of the pandemic much stronger as a community partner.

"My philosophy has been to be a servant leader. During the pandemic, there were so many unknown variables, but for the most part, we made decisions with our physicians, nurses, and clinicians 98 percent of the time. Many controversial policies and processes had to be established, and we did well together."

Matt Heinle joined NCH in the spring as general counsel for the healthcare system.

"I have a lot of healthcare clients across the country, so I was able to share what I was hearing from a lot of different providers and gave that intelligence to NCH so that they could formulate their plan," he said.

Matt immediately became immersed in the entire situation.

"NCH has a relatively small executive team. And so really the team was involved in every step of the process in terms of developing policies, pivoting with rapid change," he noted.

"It was like a spiral of activity, not just clinically to take care of the patients, but to help keep the business going because it was just chaos for many months. I think our team overall did an excellent job navigating and keeping the community educated, taking care of the community who was getting sick obviously, but then just being a good citizen of both Collier County and Naples," Matt Heinle said.

+ + +

Hardly natural allies, Lee Health of Ft. Myers and NCH histori-cally did not get along. With an annual budget now at $1.9 billion, Lee Health employs over thirteen thousand people and operates four primary hospitals that account for more than 95 percent of nearby Lee County's acute care hospital beds.

But now, alliances were being formed. It felt like choosing sides when we were kids. In picking ball players, whether you get along did not matter. If this kid was the best athlete, we'd pick that kid, even if we can't get along off the ballfield, no matter the history. This was about winning. Lee Health and NCH had a common interest now, winning against COVID-19. Both organizations had new CEOs. A real partnership developed.

LEADERSHIP TOOL KIT (PAUL)
PICKING PARTNERS

When kids play a ball game, they often line up all the players and select the coaches with a high grip on a bat. Then, the coaches take turns picking for their team. (Usually, the early picks are the best players.) If this were a game of ball, our first pick would have been Lee Health for the regional team. We would pick the big kid.

Dr. Jim Mahon ran point for joining forces with Lee Health, which launched right at the outset of COVID-19 cases in Naples and Ft. Myers.

"We became quite close and helped each other begin to think and act differently," he recalled.

Lee Health Hospital, Ft. Myers, Florida

Now, two new CEOs joined up to defeat this monster descending upon us. Earlier in the year, the first step in mending fences involved the nearby Golisano Children's Hospital, which Lee Health operates south of Fort Myers and serves seriously ill children in a five-county Southwest Florida region that includes Collier. A new transfer agreement paved the way for NCH's North Naples facility to transfer sick kids for specialty care available at Golisano, instead of Nicklaus Children's Hospital in Miami, a much closer alternative.

That positive move opened the door.

In early March, we jointly announced a restriction on visiting.

"In an effort to continue to follow the Centers for Disease Control and Prevention (CDC) guidelines and in an abundance of caution for the health and well-being for our community, we are restricting visitors at all Lee Health and NCH facilities effective immediately," our joint press release read.

"We had just closed the visitation, and I was getting pretty beat up by not allowing family to visit. The hardest thing I had ever done as a leader in this organization was not to allow visitation. Our patients were alone, and that was very hard for me. And we can only do so much with them from a virtual perspective. We have all learned the importance of family in the care of our patients."

A week later, we worked together to jointly promote establishing mobile collection sites to test patients for COVID-19. Patients must have met the specific testing criteria and had their test ordered by their physician or provider. At Lee Health patients made an appointment before visiting the collection site. NCH was not requiring appointments.

Two days later, NCH issued this press release:

FOR IMMEDIATE RELEASE NAPLES, Fla.—March 15, 2020—NCH System (NCH) has confirmation from the Florida Department of Health (FDOH) that a patient has tested positive for COVID-19.

The patient arrived at the facility on March 11 in the ER and was admitted.

NCH followed FDOH and CDC guidelines, and the patient was isolated on March 13 when the patient met the criteria for isolation. The patient is currently in isolation at an NCH facility. Federal privacy laws prevent NCH from releasing any details about our patients. FDOH is investigating travel history and opportunities for exposure and will be responsible for communicating case details, if appropriate.

"And then *bam,* COVID hit. It started slowly."

Renee Thigpen has served in human resources at NCH for decades, becoming chief human resources officer in 2015. She recalled that "we didn't know what we didn't know and what we were doing and went through the first wave."

Then, she noted, "We started to see very significant changes in the workforce with people either retiring early or getting out of the profession altogether. We saw some of the local students' applications start to decline a bit. And then our staff started leaving to take travel assignments for money, which was unbelievable."

+ + +

Five days later, Lee Health and NCH together announced that these nonprofit organizations were collaborating on all fronts, sharing policies, action plans, and daily media updates, coordinating outreach efforts, including drive-through testing sites to serve the region better, working together to limit nonurgent surgeries, and completing joint Continuing Medical Education (CME) training for team members. Together, we created the "*SWFL* (Southwest Florida) Stronger Together" campaign. The press announcement said that Lee Health and NCH asked the Southwest Florida community to join us, to come together and show support.

"*SWFL Stronger Together*" received community donations to provide critical resources, equipment, and supplies needed to support our doctors and nurses, including help providing additional ventilators, protective gear, mobile units, employee relief, and more.

Larry Antonucci, MD, MBA, the new president and CEO of Lee Health, was proud of the effort.

Larry Antonucci, MD, MBA

"During this time when COVID-19 has no borders, our organizations have collaborated in unprecedented ways. The Lee Health and NCH teams have fully embraced the concept of collaboration and community," he said in the press announcement.

Our community embraced that, and we could not help but notice that almost no one wants their healthcare providers to argue and be isolated from one another. People were weary of that. One day, we may look back and conclude that the horrible challenge of the pandemic helped heal NCH and the community. Our mobile testing events began slowly. We tested folks by appointment Monday through Friday, averaging less than forty daily tests. Patients called the centralized scheduling office Monday through Friday to set their appointments. Patients drove up to the site and remained in their cars to have samples collected by medical professionals outfitted with PPE.

As the pandemic advanced, NCH shifted personnel.

Renee Thigpen said that we tried to do everything that we could to keep people whole.

"Everybody worked if they wanted to work," she added.

"We didn't furlough anyone. For example, we repurposed wellness center staff to help in all kinds of areas, serving as our volunteers (because the volunteers weren't working), working as transporters, and in our mask clinics, or drive-in testing sites."

They shut down the childcare center and made an emergency childcare area for our frontline essential staff, including doing all the virtual training for their staff.

"We pivoted to help the employees succeed as they could while they were going through these trying times. There were a lot of unknowns. It was nice to see everyone come together and work as a team. Everybody just did whatever it took to make it work."

Because people must go so far to find affordable or available housing, critical on-call teams needed space close to the hospitals to be available. They had to arrive within minutes of a call. We rented hotel rooms close by.

In mid-March, we closed both NCH Wellness facilities until further notice to do our part to limit the spread of the disease. All memberships were put on hold.

We aggressively purchased all the personal protection gear we could find, not knowing how long this would last. We just told our supply chain staff, "Look, just get as many gloves, masks, gowns, and hats as you can find." Meanwhile, we recycled masks.

Carlos Quintero, MD

Dr. Carlos Quintero, MD, recalled that they were worried about running out of PPE and that we would resort to what many other countries were doing worldwide, using essentially plastic garbage bags, which, thankfully, we never had to get there.

"But there was that constant fear that that would potentially happen and that we would run out of masks or must utilize these masks for an extended period that was well beyond what was appropriate. The other big fear I can tell you as a physician taking care of these patients, putting all this into perspective, was the fear of bringing COVID-19 home. So what were we to do when we get home?"

"We would get home, take our clothes off outside or in the garage, throw them in the laundry, and go directly to a shower. So that was a palpable fear for us providers, the nurses, and techs. Our biggest fear was infecting our loved ones. And obviously, you saw that everywhere. That was a concern, and there were stories about people getting infected at home and people dying. So that was always a very palpable fear," Dr. Quintero added.

When tackling this emergent need, we saw the importance of partnering with our Mayo Clinic colleagues and taking advantage of their broad purchasing organization. We saw what happened in New York and bought over a hundred new ventilators. One of the major fears we all were feeling was how difficult it would be to run out of these respirators and face rationing. Nobody wanted that to happen. We ended up using only half of those.

And as time passed, we found out, *wait a minute*, that ventilators aren't necessarily the best treatment. So that was one thing we rethought. Fortunately, we had an excess of vents if another community provider needed to acquire more than they had on hand. In 2012, NCH joined the Mayo Clinic Care Network and became the first hospital in the Southeast region of the United States to do so. NCH's physicians could access Mayo Clinic physicians on patient care, community health, and innovative healthcare delivery. The expertise this decade-long relationship brought to us in the COVID-19 crisis was invaluable.

NCH benefited from the clinical leadership of Gregory Poland, MD, a professor of medicine and infectious diseases at the Mayo Clinic in Rochester, Minnesota, director of the Mayo vaccine research group, and editor-in-chief of *Vaccine*. Dr. Poland became an active member of our team, as he helped guide NCH, and the nation, through best practices during the COVID-19 pandemic. Our thorough collaboration with our doctors regarding whether to delay nonessential surgeries and which surgeries were necessary was a testament to the new world order at NCH. We made sure everyone had a say.

Dr. Poland filled Telford Auditorium for Grand Rounds, recalled Dr. Bryan Murphey.

"It was the first time in history the entire auditorium was packed with learners, community citizens, nurses, and physicians. He made himself available to us, a great resource," Dr. Murphey noted.

We announced the postponement of elective surgeries, effective March 19. This was one of many opportunities where we felt the pandemic helped us act quickly. This represented re-earning the trust of the physicians, our healthcare team, and the community leadership. The daily heroism of our clinical staff removed any remaining doubt about our value to this community.

+ + +

The notion of changing the organization's brand was often discussed. We were already changing the narrative. We were already changing the messaging, and the brand perception was rising to a new level perhaps never seen before. As the pandemic worsened, our obvious connections with Lee Health and Mayo Clinic enhanced our reputation.

We set up new platforms for the community to connect with us. For more information or to make an online donation, folks could visit SWFLtogether.org. Resources through this site also included free telehealth information, hotlines, COVID-19 news and updates, and an "Ask the Experts" forum. The healthcare systems also shared a need for blood donations, and we copromoted this as an excellent way to help and show support for our region's doctors and nurses on the front line. Our community needed fast access to the COVID-19 trends in the Naples region. Both Lee Health and NCH assembled and published a daily online update.

Both healthcare systems began serology testing, which showed the presence of COVID-19 antibodies in a patient's blood and helped us to understand how the virus spread in the region. Serology testing requires an order from the physician, and the tests could be drawn in a physician's office or at Lee Health and NCH Labs. The health systems asked people to donate blood for the Mayo Clinic COVID-19 Convalescent Plasma Study.

As the COVID-19 pandemic worsened, our dialogue with the community changed. We masked up and visited civic meetings. They welcomed us. They could not get enough information about what was going on at NCH. The toughest moment during the entire pandemic came early in the horror, the day we lost our first patient to COVID-19. Lee Health had its first loss in early March. We followed closely behind. We cannot convey the universal sadness of everyone, media included, as we faced the fact that COVID-19 would be deadly here, and that day had come.

We had so many questions we could not answer. There was so much we did not know.

On March 31, 2020, the *Naples Daily News* announced the transition from Mariann MacDonald's decade-long leadership to that of Scott Lutgert, along with best wishes because the community was counting on NCH.

The new chair of NCH, Scott Lutgert, now carried the baton.

Strong leaders coming together having different opinions? That seems very normal. But this was a COVID-19 crisis, and we needed considerable unity to get through this. Scott Lutgert brought the board together to focus and understand the serious challenges ahead, and to work together despite differences. COVID-19 was not a simple threat. We viewed it as a political discussion, with transparency, openness, and always championing the absolute necessity of their leadership. We expressed our gratitude for everything they did. To guide a major health-care system, we needed all the wisdom they have, and all the energy they could give. Things were changing fast.

> **Our "we can fix everything" self-image of American healthcare was toast. There was a life-and-death struggle going on here.**

As the storm grew, the board of trustees stepped up beautifully, asking, *"How can we help? What can we do?"* They reached out to their contacts and called on their resources to help. Because of their leadership, we never were in a sticky situation where we didn't have supplies. Community support rallied. Restaurants began sending over thousands of meals for the staff. Contributions began flowing to our fund with Lee Health. As the days passed, we began losing the sense of where the edge was. We were so busy keeping it all above water, responding to growing surges of scared and desperately ill people, that we must come up for air a bit, to take measure of where we were.

Major employers in Southwest Florida called us asking how they can help, such as Arthrex. This global medical device company is a leader in new product development and pioneered the field of arthros-copy and sports medicine. Arthrex is a privately held company; more than three thousand of its six thousand global employees are based in Collier County. It has consistently ranked among Fortune's "Top 100 Best Companies to Work For."[42]

We gasped at that air and came up with this:

---

42 Cathychestnut, "Top Employers," Southwest Florida Relocation Guide, February 26, 2021, accessed January 23, 2024, https://swflrelocationguide.com/business/top-employers/.

Our "we can fix everything" self-image of American healthcare was toast. There was a life-and-death struggle going on here. Monitor alarms and respirators' cold mechanical hum and breathy sound punctuated the tense twenty-four-hour environment. To our caregivers, it seemed never-ending. The loss of any patient was personal. There was no vaccine, and there would not be one for a long time. Our clinical team relied on their training.

The NCH team inspired us. They reminded us of the power and heroism we see in the US Armed Forces, with their total commitment and professionalism for extended periods under pressure. The horrors of the pandemic, operating at overcapacity levels, grappling with the monster desperately every minute of the day, our doctors, nurses, technicians, and staff exemplified the word "hero."

We all faced attack by this invisible death threat.

Every day, we were reminded that we could be the patient on that ventilator, alone, except for our trusted healers. They served as both caregiver and family since no visitors could be in the hospital with their loved ones. We saw this same heroism in our new community partners at other hospitals, nursing care facilities, doctors' offices, rescue squads, and police forces. While many people might be able to isolate, climb into a metaphorical cave, and watch the world's catastrophes unfold at a distance, and who could blame them, the front lines of the pandemic do not have the option of sheltering in place. We cannot abandon our patients. We cannot walk away. We did not believe that the healthcare staff would walk out. But they remain free to retire early and find another venue to use their skills.

We had steady support from our community: *We can get you one hundred thousand masks from Minnesota. We can manufacture shields for you for free.*

"And while it was frightening because there were a lot of unknown variables, I never felt like we reached the point where we did not know what to do next," said COVID-19 Task Force cochair Jon Kling, RN, "because there were so many people stepping up. In tragic situations or in stressful times, the good rises to the top."

LIVE WITH IT AND GROW NUMB

We all had a new routine when we went home, sterilizing ourselves and our garments outside our house or apartment and stepping back into our family role, praying that COVID-19 did not make a late-night visit, perhaps wishing for some symbol that could be painted above the door that made the dark visitor go past. Even with demonstrated heroism and courage every day, we were not out of the woods yet. The unfolding public health catastrophe kept getting worse. Our administrative teams planned mobile hospital expansions in the parking lot for the moment when our hospitals flared to full capacity. Based on what was happening around America, this would be soon unless we got lucky. Every day, we made it a point to acknowledge and praise the valor around us.

+ + +

When the full scope of this thing became visible, we sat down with the board and offered that it was quite possible that we could lose $60 million or more from the impact. We had to cancel elective surgeries. Hospitalizations were way down. Supply costs were soaring. They were just not rattled in the least. *We've got a balance sheet. We can handle it. Don't shortcut this place. Don't skimp on the supplies. Keep the employees safe. Avoid pay cuts.*

We teamed up with a willing community. We took part in biweekly calls to compare notes and share experiences with other providers, which included the Health Network of Southwest Florida, the Neighborhood Health Clinic, and Lee Health. We began to over-communicate. Maybe that was good or not, but we showered the leadership of Collier County and Naples, our donors, elected officials, the school boards, and the news media with information. We just communicated all over the place.

🔧 PR TOOL KIT (AMANDA)
BECOMING THE TRUSTED INFORMATION SOURCE

In a community-wide crisis, information becomes the coin of the realm. We wanted every citizen to have full access to everything we knew about this threat, and we published that daily on our NCH website. Confusing messages were coming out of national leaders. State information in Florida could have been better too. Yet the community followed our statistics every day. Sharing every bit of information, except what was not permitted due to privacy laws, was testimony that we are in full engagement with the needs of the region. Our physicians began commentary in television news appearances. We conducted media training on the fly.

Remarkably, volunteer James "Jim" Anderson posted daily data on our website for us every day for over a year. Every morning, he updated all the statistics on COVID-19 at NCH and around the state so that the community could have full access when they signed on. Jim's background in accounting led the way, and we became a trusted source for COVID-19 information.

Looking back, as we made important decisions, there was always room for debate. Everyone had different views on such matters as visiting rules, masking rules, and many challenging changes to consider. But we usually noticed that we made quicker decisions than many other providers, probably because we set up a streamlined process and quickly addressed physician issues at the outset. We made decisions before they were popular. News media discussion of how NCH made decisions and how we managed this community resource took a back seat to COVID-19. The pandemic gave us a new platform to appear at powerful local civic groups with some up-to-the-minute inside information about how the healthcare world dealt with this.

We spoke to many groups in the community, such as Rotary and Kiwanis Clubs. Our top executives spoke at dozens of community gatherings. We rekindled a very strong connection with the leadership of the Chamber of Commerce. Every week, someone was speaking somewhere in the community. Former chief nursing officer Jonathan Kling, RN (since promoted to Chief Operating Officer of the System [COO]), recalled going with Paul to civic groups. "What I saw with Paul was that he was very consistent when he spoke to people, it wasn't like he was reading from *PowerPoint*. It wasn't rehearsed. It was open and human, and I saw people gravitate toward him. The message was, OK, we can talk about the past, but what can we do together differently from now on? And everywhere I went with him, I saw healing, which was cool, because I was there through the tough times."

✦ ✦ ✦

In our report to the board of trustees just before the pandemic hit, we summarized our accomplishments over the first six months at NCH. We agreed to new cardiology physician relationships.

We restructured marketing and communications. Donors had begun to return. NCH began regular press briefings with a prescheduled call time. Any news media member could join the call and this routine practice opened critical lines of communication with the public. We also let all the reporters know that interviews had to be arranged outside or away from the facilities for safety.

"I made a commitment to be on the phone with Paul and my editorial board every week," said *Naples Daily News* publisher Bill Barker.

"And they committed to be there as well. I would imagine that there's no other hospital or newspaper in the country that can say that they sat down every week and gave the community an update through this pandemic. And I'm talking about the hospital's CEO and the newspaper's CEO sitting down with their teams, telling the community what's going on with this pandemic. I bet that's unprecedented," Barker noted.

Barker tipped his hat to Amanda and Paul. "We had this disruption about this healthcare organization, and then the transition and fallout, but then the pandemic layers on top of that."

"Now you have a community that needs this organization to be stable and to be ahead of the game. Amanda was here and ready when Paul arrived. She was clearly needed when the pandemic hit on top of everything else. I mean, think about the layering."

Beginning on March 30, 2020, the US Department of Health and Human Services (HHS) started a program they coined *"Operation Warp Speed,"* to expedite a COVID-19 vaccine. Significant funding was authorized for vaccine research and development. HHS also fundamentally changed how pharmaceutical and biotechnology companies assess the risk of conducting large-scale clinical trials on new vaccines. They also guaranteed manufacture and purchased allotments of the vaccines in advance whether any of the funded companies would be successful.[43]

On April 1, 2020, Paul spoke to the news media on *Zoom*. We did a number of these Zoom meetings throughout the year, totaling thousands of participants in small groups from all over Collier County and Naples.

"Hello Again, Friends. This Is Paul Hiltz, CEO of NCH"

Well, COVID-19 has certainly changed our lives, hasn't it? In just a matter of days, not weeks, we've gone from being vigilant and diligently washing our hands to self-isolation and social distancing.

Everyone is on high alert as this pandemic has hit not only our nation but our planet hard. Life is not the same. Our grocery stores are quiet with empty shelves and our beaches are empty. Many of our shops and restaurants are either closed or have limited availability.

And while the practice of social distancing has created precautionary distance from one another to help the spread of our virus, it's created a giant void in our daily lives.

It's eliminated hugs from friends and handshakes, from neighbors. It's separated families and isolated friends, warm interactions, and quality time that we human beings so desperately need.

I understand this isn't news to any of you, but it's an awkward and unexpected reality. We're now living to keep our communities well, but in every challenge, every unfortunate circumstance, we

---

43   Brothers, "A Timeline of COVID-19 Vaccine Development."

have hope. That's what I want to talk to you about today. What is our opportunity for hope during this COVID-19 crisis? You know, when I took this job back in September 2019, one of the attractions was the power of this community.

The passion and commitment of the community in Southwest Florida is special. Since then, I've met with hundreds of you. You've graciously welcomed me into your businesses and your homes. The way you've rallied around this healthcare system.

The way you've rallied around this healthcare system and the progress we've made has been invigorating. We feed off of the energy in the community. Well, I'm here to tell you that COVID-19 can't shake the power of this community.

🔧 LEADERSHIP TOOL KIT (PAUL)
SINCERITY

If we reread that letter, with an eye on the sincerity and belief in the organization, it becomes clear that encouragement and gratitude go a long way in a crisis. We always thanked the community for its efforts to keep everyone safe. He held several events to thank the support team sincerely and personally, usually with free ice cream, for their tough, continuous work. It's not what you say so much as how you say it. Sincerity is the doorway to good leadership when things get tough.

The board of trustees played a vital role in confronting this new crisis.

Michael Wynn of our board penned a beautiful "Perspectives" Opinion piece, which appeared in the *Naples Daily News* on April 22, 2020.[44]

> COVID-19 has turned all our lives upside down. There are many on the front lines that deserve our praise. First and foremost are the nurses and doctors who knowingly put themselves at risk to protect us. The spotlight is justifiably on them and all they are doing to keep us safe. This event has pulled back the curtain to reveal the talented men and women who have always been there for us, waiting to help when we need it most...
>
> With all the focus on PPE, testing, and the valid concerns over exposure to the coronavirus, we forget about all the emotional investment that our healthcare workers make in their patients each day. That takes a heavy toll on them without having to also shoulder a global pandemic. They are truly lifesaving heroes that deserve our gratitude and respect now and in the future.

The global pandemic has impacted our overall economy, and NCH is no exception. We have seen a dramatic decrease in inpatient and outpatient volume.

---

44   Michael Wynn, "Opinion: NCH Is a Lifesaver, Then and Now," *Naples Daily News*, April 22, 2020, accessed September 1, 2021, https://www.naplesnews.com/story/opinion/contributors/2020/04/22/opinion-nch-lifesaver-then-and-now/3003720001/.

In these tough economic times, NCH maintained essential clinical staff levels to prepare and combat COVID-19, while continually assessing our workforce needs to shift resources where they are needed most.

In pursuit of that effort, we closed or reduced many of our impacted departments and have repurposed as many employees as possible to other job duties at their current base compensation. Clinical staff were retrained and repositioned to help in our critical care, respiratory, and COVID-19 units, or act as relief for our staff already there. Additionally, we continued to "staff to volume" in all areas and have adjusted schedules, and many of our staff members in the nonclinical areas are reducing their hours by a minimum of one day per pay period, to further manage the financial challenges this pandemic has caused.

Thankfully, NCH has received tremendous community support, and we've received $12 million in donations for the fiscal year. Over $4 million of that total was raised in March. In addition, we've received over one hundred pledges that arrived in the mail in response to our direct mail appeal. We applied for the Federal Stimulus Hospital Relief Package and have received advanced Medicare payments that have improved our financial position. NCH maintained a strong financial position, and we were prepared to get through this pandemic fiscally sound. Planning to reallocate resources and be fiscally responsible during COVID-19 will better position us once this pandemic ends.

Frequently, we updated the employees with details on our financial posture and explanations for the necessary spending restraint.

🔧 LEADERSHIP TOOL KIT (PAUL)
LANGUAGE FOR LEADERS IN CRISIS

In his book, best-selling author Erik Larson examines the determination of the "British Bulldog" during England's darkest hour. We read that book. Larson tells the powerful story of a defiant prime minister who almost single-handedly willed his nation to resist. *The Splendid and the Vile: A Saga of Churchill, Family, and Defiance During the Blitz* examines a leader in crisis—a challenge of epic proportions with the fate of democracy hanging in the balance. Knowing that the language of leadership is critical, we found this was very inspirational because, during the darkest hours of the London bombings, he didn't say, *Oh, this will be over soon.* All he said was "We're going to get through it." We tried to take a page from that book and said, basically: *We don't know how long this is going to go, but we're not going to run out of beds, we're not going to run out of PPE, and we will eventually get through it. We'll have to figure out when that's going to be, but until then, let's keep together.*

The tougher it got, the more we tried to be visible on all three shifts. We put the right team in place and empowered them to make decisions. You can't micromanage during a crisis. You've got to say, *This is where we're going, so go.* Now we can run faster. But we also didn't make decisions in a silo. We led decision-making and empowered our team. No edicts. We worked collaboratively to make sure they were listening to the voice of the physicians and listening to the clinicians.

The *Naples Daily News* reported in a retrospective article on Dr. David Lindner that this powerful NCH physician "knew COVID-19 was uncharted territory when he embarked on the biggest challenge of his career."

David Lindner, MD

"As medical director of the COVID-19 response team at the NCH System, all eyes were on him for how he would help the 713-bed system, the largest in Collier County, get ready for the airborne virus," the newspaper *reported*.[45]

When he accepted the job in early March 2019, he was already on high alert, brought on by his knowledge of how pandemics take root. Naples had yet to see any confirmed cases—that would come on

---

45   Liz Freeman, "How Did NCH's COVID-19 Team Leader Win Physician of the Year? By Focusing on What's Best for Patients," *Naples Daily News*, March 5, 2021, accessed March 13, 2024, https://www.naplesnews.com/story/news/2021/03/05/covid-19-leader-nch-physician-year-dr-david-lindner-reflects-pandemic/4539159001/.

March 11—but he knew the tourism hotspot with loads of well-heeled international travelers and happy-go-lucky retirees sitting inches apart in jammed restaurants was ripe for a catastrophe. The *Naples Daily News* reported that more than two hundred twenty-six thousand visitors had stayed in commercial lodgings in February 2020.[46]

Dr. Lindner, board certified in pulmonary medicine, internal medicine, and critical care medicine and heads up NCH's ICUs, knew there was no clinical data, research, or patient care protocols for COVID-19.

"The scary part was how people immediately assumed I was an expert," said Dr. Lindner. ("There were no experts," he noted.)

His cochair of the COVID-19 Task Force, Jonathan Kling, RN, agreed.

"I remember our first press conference. People were asking me so many questions and expected me to know what I was doing and what I was saying, and I was terrified that I would say something wrong and hurt somebody."

Dr. Carlos Quintero noted that many of the nursing staff volunteered to take care of the COVID-19 units. They were willing to be in harm's way, and they were willing to work twelve-hour shifts only with COVID-19 patients. We often see nurses racing to a clinical emergency and rushing into a patient's room without being fully protected.

"The ICU team and the respiratory therapists were involved day in and day out with patients requiring intubation, requiring negative pressure ventilation (which essentially puts you at higher risk for aerosol infection)."

---

46   Laura Layden, "Tourism in Collier County Breaks Records in 2019,"
      Naples Daily News, January 28, 2020, accessed March 14, 2020, https://
      www.naplesnews.com/story/money/business/local/2020/01/28/
      collier-county-saw-record-tourism-2019/4587666002/.

"Our Quality team also dealt with the hazards of moving patients around the hospital. We did our best to cohort COVID-19 patients in units, but inevitably, they would need to be moved around for x-rays or therapy. A huge challenge for us. And what about family members of our patients? How can we help them avoid infection?" Dr. Quintero added.

NCH's peak volume for admitted patients with COVID-19 during 2020 was July 15 with 144 patients. The *Naples Daily News* also reported that Dr. Lindner would be recognized as Physician of the Year. "Because of his work on the COVID-19 team and other leadership roles in the pulmonary and critical care programs, plus his tenure on the medical staff since 1994," said Dr. Doug Harrington, who specializes in pulmonary medicine and critical care medicine at NCH.

Doug Harrington, MD

Dr. Paul Jones, a member of the COVID-19 response team until his term ended as president of the medical staff, said Dr. Lindner was instrumental in getting physicians ready to care for infected patients and was tireless in his research.

"COVID-19 is a very complex thing, and we came up very rapidly," Dr. Jones said. "It gave us confidence as providers."

The *Naples Daily News* reported that Dr. Lindner spearheaded NCH's involvement in clinical studies, including for remdesivir and convalescent plasma, two treatments that were since approved, Dr. Jones said.

"He also helped us decide what not to use," Dr. Jones said, citing the drug hydroxychloroquine that was in the national limelight. Then-President Donald Trump tweeted and talked about the anti-malaria drug as a treatment despite what top health experts said was no evidence it benefits COVID-19 patients.

"It turns out Dr. Lindner was right," Dr. Jones said. "In the internet world, there is a lot of unfettered information, and Dr. Lindner helped us sort through a lot of that noise."

Dr. Harrington told the newspaper that because of Dr. Lindner's leadership, the critical care division established patient care protocols in the early months of the pandemic.

"We were well ahead of the curve," Dr. Harrington said. "We were months ahead of other hospital organizations."

Dr. Lindner's cochair Jonathan Kling, RN, had known him since 2003 when he started in the surgical ICU. Then he became the medical director and the critical care director in 2007.

"Dr. Lindner walked up to me and took a close look. He said, 'Jon, you need to take some time off. I'm worried about you.'"

Then he made Jon take two days off.

We began working with key doctors from the onset of COVID-19, coaching them to become great spokespersons. It became apparent from the outset that we needed prepared physicians to be willing and able to go on TV, comfortably talk about the pandemic and the hospital, and communicate what the public was being requested to do. The words "willing and able" were somewhat hard to come by. During a public health crisis, the community needed trustworthy physicians to reassure them. Both Dr. Harrington and Dr. Lindner became household names during the pandemic.

PR TOOL KIT (AMANDA)
MEDIA TRAINING IN ADVANCE

Every organization needs to have an on-camera spokesperson. And everyone, regardless of how confident, needs interactive practice for broadcast as well as print media. We asked several doctors to join us for some formal media training. Some of our doctors, especially those that had been in the community for a while, seeing all the negative press, had a terrible opinion of the media. They did not want to do it. But we explained that this was important. Being a spokesperson in COVID-19 was just a first step to representing the excellence of your specialty. Keeping sound bites relevant, brief, and answering even combative questions politely, with clarity, takes some practice to do well.

At first, we did some informal guidance just before an interview, or whenever we could collar the doctors. Finally, we asked for a whole day of their time for training, a very difficult request of a physician, even in normal times. But they did and were very pleased with the new skills they developed. The full-day training familiarizes the person with anything the media can throw at you. The anxiety dissipates. Do the training before you need it. You will need it. But there may be an unintended outcome. It seems that the more you train for this kind of thing, the more opportunities rise to use that training.

By midsummer, Moderna and Pfizer, both of which used the mRNA vaccine approach, became the leaders in the race to develop a COVID-19 vaccine. Moderna published initial Phase I/II clinical trial data on July 14, Pfizer in August. The results demonstrated promising safety measures and antibody production against the spike protein from those who got the vaccine.[47]

One of the successful initiatives we were most proud of in 2020 was the improvement in quality measures of the hospital, despite the challenge of the pandemic. We always hold onto the continuing drive for accountability for quality, following protocols, and doing the absolute best we can on every quality measure. We built a data infrastructure called a data warehouse. We needed to make sure we had the metrics. You need to measure it to improve it. Our focus on quality led us to higher patient experience and safety scores even during the pandemic. The toughest problem was staffing, just keeping staff, hiring staff, and getting that right. We needed to improve our staff retention, but it just kept getting harder as the pandemic surge stretched everything we had.

Jonathan Kling, RN, said, "We lost about 210 nurses to traveling nurse agencies and clinical staff who left us. We were able to continue to hire during the pandemic. We struggled like everybody else, but at our peak, we had eighty-eight travelers, which was a lot for us."

---

47   Will Brothers, "A Timeline of COVID-19 Vaccine Development."

We were not immune to the loss of nurses during this time, as were hospitals nationwide. Some great nurses just withdrew and went home to care for their families.

Even though NCH at one point had hundreds of patients hospitalized with COVID-19, the system did not stop strategic projects. These include starting the move to a new electronic medical record (EMR) with Epic, costing $100 million, expanding its cardiac care and pediatrics programs, and the ongoing $30 million upgrade of the NCH Downtown Baker Hospital emergency room. As we marched along, the news about the vaccine breakthroughs lifted everyone's spirits.

How Millions of Lives Were Saved by Science

From my point of view, the development, testing, and approval of a vaccine for COVID-19 under Operation Warp Speed is unprecedented in the history of the drug (vaccine) development process in the United States.

—Richard Zakour, PhD

We interviewed Dr. Richard Zakour, who recently retired from a four-decade high-level career in worldwide logistics for clinical trials for vaccine development and distribution. His concise play-by-play of the miraculous development of an effective vaccine for COVID-19 has been enlightening.

"Typically, the process of developing a new vaccine in the United States takes five to ten years or more," he said, "with many factors going into this process, including foundational basic research, animal testing models, comparison to similar products, such as previously approved vaccines, and lots and lots of testing at many levels."

To put it quite simply, he noted, any new product approved by the *Food and Drug Administration* (FDA) must pass a barrage of feasibility, safety, and preliminary efficacy (how well does it work) tests before it can ever begin to be truly studied in humans.

"This is a very long and laborious process," Dr. Zakour noted.

"To begin with, there is often some prior history in the development of any vaccine. Specifically, approved vaccines for similar viruses or other diseases may already exist and thus provide a model to approach the development of a new vaccine product. The target (virus) of the vaccine may typically be well known, often from years of scientific research studies.

"COVID-19 is a member of a class of viruses known as coronaviruses that mainly cause respiratory and gastrointestinal infections in humans, including the common cold, and infects a wide variety of other mammals.

"There are tried and true methods for the development of vaccines that have been around for a century or more," he explained.

"For example, the use of live and/or inactivated attenuated viruses and viral proteins, as in the case of smallpox and polio vaccines as well as many more recent products, have been widely used in developing many viral vaccines. In the case of COVID-19, two companies, Pfizer and Moderna, were attempting to develop novel vaccines based on relatively new technology using messenger RNA (mRNA).

"The idea of using mRNA to produce a vaccine is innovative and is based on a very simple principle. Specifically, the goal was to use the body's cells to incorporate injected mRNA and have the body produce antibodies to an attacking foreign substance (such as COVID-19).

"Briefly, mRNA is the product that the body naturally produces and uses to translate the genetic code from the DNA to make the proteins that cells need for virtually everything that they do, including fighting foreign invaders.

"So, the principle would be to inject synthetic mRNA into the body to have the cells of the body produce proteins (in this case, antibodies) that would be effective in countering the attack of foreign substances such as a Coronavirus (the family of viruses that includes COVID-19).

"Although relatively easy and quick to produce compared to traditional vaccine-making processes, no mRNA vaccine or drug has ever won approval by the FDA.

"Although research has been ongoing for over twenty years on mRNA-produced products in cellular and animal models, testing at the human level has been minimal, not to mention using the process to develop an effective product for mass production and administration in humans.

"With the rapidly evolving COVID-19 pandemic starting in 2020, it became extremely urgent to develop effective vaccines to contain this virus and curtail its spread. Thus, several organizations worldwide embarked on this objective.

"Many approaches were needed, including developing experimental products such as the novel mRNA vaccine model, as well as traditional models (attenuated viruses) for developing vaccines to counter this deadly menace."

Dr. Zakour was adamant that the speed and efficiency of doing this could only be possible with a "wartime" effort on the part of the federal government such as Operation Warp Speed. As an all-out approach to combating the pandemic, various companies used a variety of vaccine development models.

"This could only be done under the auspices of the US government to facilitate this gigantic process by basically underwriting the enormous cost of such a project."

As of this writing, he observed, the objective to develop and produce a variety of novel vaccines on such an accelerated time scale must be deemed an overall huge success. Two mRNA-based vaccines and one viral-based vaccine (Johnson and Johnson) received emergency and/or final approval from the FDA.

"This approval is a very rigorous process and, as stated previously, takes many years. In the case of COVID-19 vaccines, it has taken less than one year."

Dr. Zakour also noted that other vaccines are in the pipeline as well as continuing studies on the side effects and possible long-term effects of these new products in humans.

"However, the results to date certainly validate the effectiveness of the vaccines that have been used based on the curtailment of the progression of COVID-19 infections and deaths."

Richard A. Zakour, PhD, is the retired general manager of McKesson (now Thermo Fisher) BioServices, a subsidiary specializing in logistics for clinical trial supplies serving pharmaceutical companies, the National Institute of Allergy and Infectious Diseases, the National Cancer Institute, and the US Army. Dr. Zakour trained as a molecular biologist and cancer research scientist at Rice University and the University of Washington, and he also served as executive director of the MdBio Division of the Technology Council of Maryland.

MASKING UP

During the first calm moment in months, we began designing what we believed was an almost perfect collaborative public campaign with the City of Naples about the pandemic. We stepped into it with the thought of a thank you campaign for our heroic caregivers. Then we realized that much work needed to be done to promote mask-wearing. Floridians, for the most part, resist being told what to do. The City of Naples, Collier County, and the school systems were vacillating about mandatory masking. Elected officials were bouncing back and forth as well. Everyone wanted to do the right thing. They couldn't agree on what the right thing was. Some Florida citizens agreed that mask-wearing may be a good idea but that the government should not make it mandatory. Hefty fines and the enforcement complications also left a bad taste in everyone's mouth.

During the pandemic, you rarely knew who was behind the mask saving your life, but they would be providing love and comfort in an isolation room. This affected the rich and poor. With COVID-19, there has yet to be class distinction. The doctor, nurse, or technician in the hospital behind the mask knew that their patients probably could not identify them as a person. They willingly accepted the anonymity of the caregiver, eyes only, no facial expression, and the task of trying to let their patients know that despite this, there was a caring, loving human being next to them, doing their job.

In public, we rarely knew who was behind the mask-wearing citizen going to the grocery store. But it did say to us, *I care for you; therefore, I am wearing this to protect you from the unspeakable hazard we all face.*

The City of Naples was in a posture of trying to help, to do something about masking. That could well become a campaign of encouragement. Our partners at the City helped us create a City of Naples-NCH campaign designed to last three to four months. The program evolved into a full-scale comprehensive educational initiative encouraging mask-wearing, physical distancing, and best hygiene practices to fight COVID-19 with the theme:

"It's our responsibility to help save lives. Wear a mask. Be a hero."

We could help solve a mask-wearing problem by broad, highly visible public encouragement of mask use. This would have a side benefit of demonstrating our community loyalty enhancing NCH, the City, and the business community. We could elevate and publicly recognize the heroes in healthcare, our caregivers, and make stars of City workers and other people who voluntarily wear masks to protect each other, with the same beautiful thought:

We purposefully didn't say social distancing because during this pandemic, our social connections were more important than ever … so we said physical distancing.

The Great Mask Giveaway

Dr. Jim Mahon led governmental relations for NCH as well as philanthropy. He described the excellent early working relationship with Mayor Theresa Heitmann. Then Amanda and her team put together a great program and marketing campaign, he noted.

Over our two years of fighting COVID-19, "NCH and the City of Naples gave away 1.3 million masks. We'd give everybody a box of fifty," he said.

It was already sealed, totally sanitized, he noted. We never gave an individual mask. We gave a box of fifty to everybody. "We'd give out two hundred thousand masks at a farmers market on a Saturday morning," he recalled.

We dropped over boxes of masks at the airport, restaurants, hotels, churches, city facilities, the airports, and businesses throughout Collier County. Everywhere we went, we carried boxes of masks. City council joined us as well as city employees and first responders. We delivered a lot of masks out in Immokalee, the area where many migrant farm workers live. We gave lots of PPE there because there was a huge spike in COVID-19.

We had a common foe now. During the first thirty days, the leadership filmed a series of public service announcements, publishing them on "Zoom" and other outlets. Chamber of Commerce CEO Michael Darby appeared for the joint events.

Dr. Quintero kept a close eye on disadvantaged farm workers during the crisis.

"I'm originally from Panama, and I have a keen interest in disadvantaged patient populations. The Hispanic migrants in the nearby town of Immokalee was a hotspot because either the patients did not believe in COVID-19 or they did not know enough about it," he recalled.

Dr. Quintero recorded interviews and public service messages in Spanish, pleading with them to follow the basic techniques to prevent infection, hand hygiene, the distancing, and masks. One interview on a Hispanic radio station lasted well over an hour.

"And what was astonishing to me early on was that because the employers required them to continue to work on the farms, they were getting infected at work and taking all these infections to their homes, which were densely populated, such as two-bedroom apartments housing ten people. They either had to work, or they lost their job.

"We could clearly see the differences in socioeconomic status. A lot of young people were dying, their entire family infected."

Videos and photographs of Naples community members wearing masks (moms, grandfathers, kids, police officers, bakers, construction workers, firefighters, etc.) in prominent locations in Naples were created. They were displayed in multiple media: online, ads, banners, the city's pole banners, and displays at the airport. NCH and the city shared the media budget. Businesses displayed the materials willingly.

The elected officials and city staff joined us in giving out free masks at public events and venues and offering masks in larger quantities for businesses. Thousands of masks were given away every week on our websites. Dr. Jim Mahon observed that the thing that helped flip the whole image of NCH, as much as anything, he said, was the leadership role the health system played in protecting this community through COVID-19. *All Heroes Wear Masks* was an integral part of why we are enjoying some of the benefits we have today with the community.

+ + +

A sigh of relief ...

In Pfizer's Phase III trial, there were 170 confirmed cases of COVID-19, 162 of which occurred in the placebo arm. That's an efficacy rate of approximately 95 percent. Furthermore, they reported an extremely low number (less than 2 percent) of adverse events, none of which required immediate or critical medical attention.

It was beginning to look like the original model for healthcare in America, the three-legged stool of government, hospital, and community as envisioned by Benjamin Franklin and Thomas Bond, would be the white horse that we rode to rescue a nation in shutdown and fear.

Similarly, Moderna's efficacy rate was approximately 95 percent, where the number of symptomatic COVID-19 cases in the treatment arm of the trial was only eleven compared to the 185 cases in the placebo arm. Significantly, while thirty of the 185 cases in the placebo arm developed into a severe case of COVID-19 requiring hospitalization, zero such cases were found in the vaccine arm. These results suggest that Moderna's vaccine protects against infection and potentially protects against developing severe cases of the disease.

Both Pfizer and Moderna sent these successful efficacy results to the US FDA for Emergency Use Authorization (EUA). Vaccine doses would be available for use twenty-four to seventy-two hours after FDA approval. Moderna hoped to have twenty million doses available by the end of 2020, with Pfizer saying that fifty million doses of their vaccine will be available globally by then.

By late summer, with the continuing support of Mayo Clinic's Dr. Gregory Poland, we were learning more about this new vaccine technology. We were in awe that this miracle may save millions of lives, starting this year, not years from now. We were especially optimistic that its development would finally give significant protection for our caregivers. The light at the end of the tunnel was visible; it was not a train, and our moods improved.

It was beginning to look like the original model for healthcare in America; the three-legged stool of government, hospital, and community, as envisioned by Benjamin Franklin and Thomas Bond, would be the white horse that we rode to rescue a nation in shutdown and fear.

We pinched ourselves. The fastest vaccine on record took four years, while most vaccines take over a decade to test and bring to market. The government stepped up. We stepped up. The community stepped up. Using funding from generous community donors, NCH began prepping for the vaccine. We made a rapid decision to purchase ultra-cold freezers as soon as we learned that the Pfizer vaccine would require super-cold storage. That turned out to be prescient because the demand would vastly outpace the supply.

In the summer of 2020, we entered the worst part of the COVID-19 crisis thus far. In August, we peaked in new cases per day. This vaccine could not come soon enough. Everybody was just exhausted. They were fighting mask fatigue. Generally, our caregivers are warm, caring people, but the COVID-19 patients could only have minimal contact. That was frustrating. Patients' families were not allowed to visit. It was just dehumanizing, and the stress level was ratcheted to full power every minute of the day for the physicians, nurses, and hospital staff.

Despite all the setbacks and the day-to-day tension, we promised ourselves that we would fight the pandemic but keep track of where we are going as regards quality of care, technology, and clinical development. We leaned into our long-term plan and kept things in motion when many would have tabled decisions until the crisis was over.

One of the facts of life of America's healthcare is competition. That can be good as providers compete in the marketplace to become the hospital of choice. The reward is more patients, higher revenues, a greater ability to attract and retain great doctors, nurses, and clinicians. Unlike many nations with universal care, competition makes the clock tick.

"The debut of open-heart surgery at the Pine Ridge campus of nearby Physicians Regional ushered in a new era in Collier County for patients to have another option for where to have the lifesaving surgery close to home," reported the *Naples Daily News*.[48]

NCH had run the only program in Collier since 1996. Paul Hiltz wished the new open-heart team the best. Several clinicians had previously worked at NCH. We needed more time and energy to fret about whether it was in the community's best interest to have a duplication of service. We were fighting a pandemic. But we did recognize the need to ramp up the information going out to the community about our long-standing open-heart program and the NCH Heart Institute.

We launched a beautiful campaign highlighting our heart program. The NCH Heart Institute provides award-winning services in cardiology and electrophysiology and home to the first open-heart surgery program in Collier County.

The NCH Heart Institute has become proficient in comprehensive cardiac care to prevent, treat, and cure cardiovascular disease. We have been recognized for our *Code Save-A-Heart* Program, open-heart surgery, cutting-edge technology, quality physicians and staff, outstanding outcomes, and consistently high patient satisfaction ratings.

48   Liz Freeman, "Physicians Regional Healthcare System Begins open-Heart Surgery," *Naples Daily News*, July 20, 2020, accessed November 15, 2021, https://www.naplesnews.com/story/news/health/2020/07/30/physicians-regional-debuts-open-heart-surgery-help-address-growth/5521595002/.

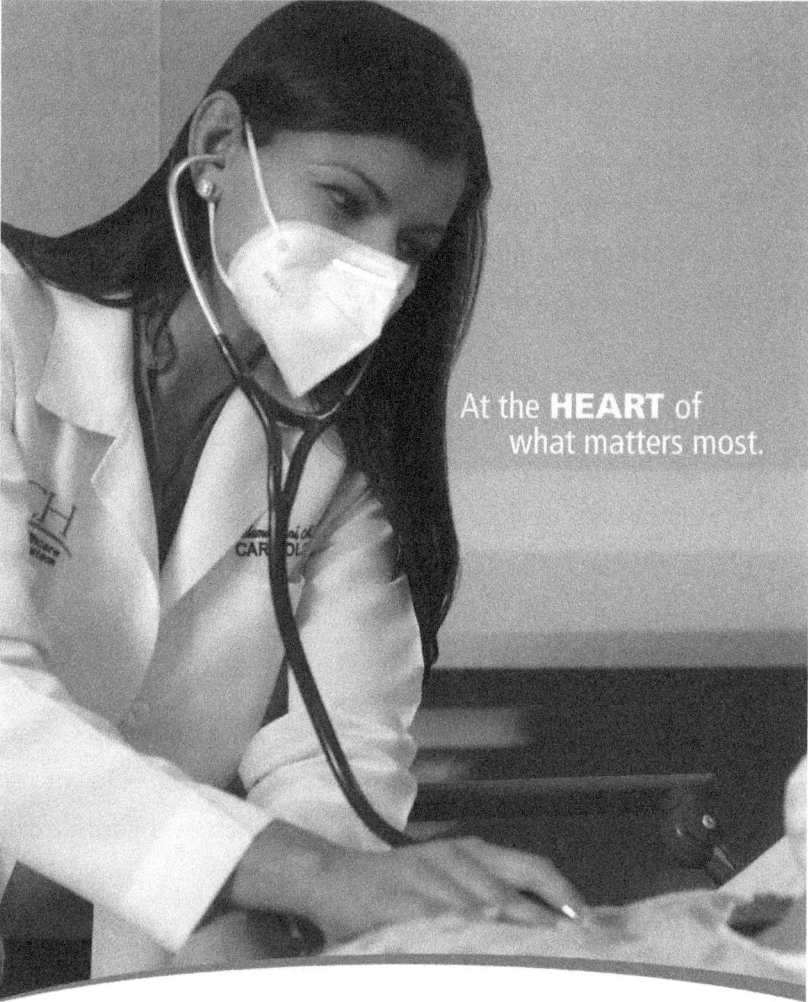

At the **HEART** of
what matters most.

NCH
Heart
Institute

The Difference Is In the Care.
At NCH Heart Institute, compassionate care is at
the heart of what matters most. From diagnosis to
recovery, our renowned physicians and nurses provide
a comprehensive cardiac care experience that is
unparalleled and had led NCH to be named as one of
America's 100 best hospitals for cardiac care.

NCHheart.com

Generous community support enabled NCH to implement
the Watchman program for patients with atrial fibrillation and offer
the latest valve repair and replacement. We also stayed on course to

advance our EMR system and prepared to launch a new system in the coming months at a cost of nearly $100 million. The new Epic system was planned to take effect the next year. We kept going with the Epic acquisition planning and were still on target, which was terrific.

We never stopped forward momentum, ever. We began an internal recognition program called "Above and Beyond," which helped the employees remember how much they were appreciated.

- *On December 11, 2020, the FDA issued an EUA for the use of the Pfizer-BioNTech COVID-19 vaccine.*[49]
- *On December 18, 2020, the FDA issued an EUA for the use of the Moderna COVID-19 vaccine.*
- *On February 27, 2021, the FDA issued an EUA for the use of the Janssen COVID-19 vaccine. The issuance of an EUA differs from FDA approval (licensure) of a vaccine.*

On December 18, 2020, our Leapfrog scores went from a C to an A at the North Naples facility and from a D to a B at the Downtown Baker facility. We also received the nation's highest rating for cardiac surgery.

"Our goal is to strive for an exceptional patient experience each and every time, and this ranking from Leapfrog is yet another accolade to add to our growing list of awards recognizing NCH for the quality and safe care we provide," we said in a statement.

49   Will Brothers, "A Timeline of COVID-19 Vaccine Development."

Bill Barker Steps Down

The Season of Hope had a melancholy moment when *Naples Daily News* publisher Bill Barker stepped down from his post on December 16, 2020. This was a huge loss. In his time in Southwest Florida as a newspaper executive, Barker said he's had many proud moments on the job—and in the community. His priorities have been to help strengthen the community and to help businesses grow, while representing the newspaper industry and standing up for freedom of the press.[50]

"Nothing is about any one person," he said. "All I do is stand in front and represent a very important institution here." He's proud of the stories that have changed people's lives, the editorials that have helped and informed the community, and the sales and advertising teams that supported the journalistic mission.

In mid-December, we received the best news possible. NCH was among 173 hospitals statewide that were notified by federal officials that it would receive the Moderna vaccine after it had gained emergency authorization for use. We quickly explained the federal protocols to the community. Even though the vaccine was arriving, the community needed to continue wearing masks, social distancing, and washing their hands frequently, which have been the main preventive tools for ten months since the pandemic began. They had

---

50   Laura Layden, "Bill Barker Steps Down as Publisher in SWFL, Regional President for Gannett," *Naples Daily News*, December 16, 2020, accessed November 21, 2021, naplesnews.com/story/money/business/local/2020/12/16/bill-barker-steps-down-publisher-regional-president-gannett-southwest-florida/3913168001/.

to understand that we must protect the caregivers first, those in direct contact with COVID-19 patients.

Dr. David Lindner explained to the *Naples Daily News* that high-risk medical staff would be the first recipients. Once NCH finishes vaccinating its high-risk medical staff, the system will spread out to vaccinate other staff and doctors who have registered to get it, Lindner said. NCH has nine hundred physicians on staff. About 1,800 employees were considered frontline workers who come into contact daily with COVID-19, according to Dr. Lindner. The hospital did not yet expect to receive a supply of the Pfizer vaccine. The first allocation through the state was the Moderna vaccine, which did not require ultra-cold storage.

THE BEST DAY EVER AT NCH

The atmosphere was electric throughout the organization.

Dr. Carlos Quintero explained that the vaccination topic was difficult because there was "little that we *knew* about the vaccines, but we knew that they would help."

"We didn't know how much, and we didn't know what the side effects would be. So it was very challenging to put mandates or policies in place with little information. That's just something you normally don't have to do; you rely on a lot of data, previous studies, and best practices to put policies and mandates in place. So it was very challenging, but in the end, we were trying to do what we thought was best at the time."

Lady Mary Wortley Montague

In Asia, practitioners developed the technique of variolation—the deliberate infection with smallpox. Dried smallpox scabs were blown into the nose of an individual who then contracted a mild form of the disease. Upon recovery, the individual was immune to smallpox. Between 1 and 2 percent of those variolated died as compared to 30 percent who died when they contracted the disease naturally.[51]

By 1700, variolation had spread to Africa, India, and the Ottoman Empire. In contrast to Asians and Africans who inoculated by blowing dried smallpox scabs up the nose, Europeans and their American cousins tended to inoculate through skin punctures.

In 1717, Lady Mary Wortley Montague, the wife of the British ambassador, learned about variolation in Constantinople. In 1721, at the urging of Montagu and the Princess of Wales, several prisoners and abandoned children were inoculated by having smallpox inserted under the skin. Several months later, the children and prisoners were deliberately exposed to smallpox. When none contracted the disease, the procedure was deemed safe, and members of the royal family were inoculated. The procedure then became fashionable in Europe.

Cotton Maher, a minister in Boston, reports that his servant Onesimus had undergone the procedure as a child in what is now southern Liberia, Africa. Moreover, two Welsh doctors, Perrot Williams and Richard Wright, reported that inoculation

---

51   National Library of Medicine, "History of Medicine," accessed March 14, 2024, https://www.nlm.nih.gov/exhibition/smallpox/sp_variolation.html.

was well known in Wales and had been practiced there since at least 1600.

Regardless of geographical origin, the story of inoculation eventually led to one of the greatest medical achievements of humankind: the eradication of smallpox in 1980. And of course, it inspired the development of vaccines for many more infectious diseases, turning this planet into a much safer place.[52]

"December 23, 2020, was the most euphoric day in healthcare in my entire career," Paul told the employees assembled to give the first immunizations.

NCH received 4,900 doses of the Moderna vaccine, and frontline healthcare workers lined up to get their first dose in the fight against COVID-19.

"So many people have worked tirelessly to bring the vaccine to market, and we are extremely grateful," Paul said at the media event. "We all hope this will be the beginning of the end of this global pandemic."

Lynda Pike, who started at NCH that July, was the first employee to get the vaccine. Pike, a respiratory therapist who works with COVID-19 patients, said she was honored to be the first.[53]

"It's a huge relief because it releases some of the tension," she said. "We have worked in the front lines. (Now) we are less vulnerable."

---

52 Ibid.

53 Liz Freeman, "High Risk Healthcare Workers at NCH Get First Dose," *Naples Daily News*, December 3, 2020, accessed November 15, 2021, https://www.naplesnews. com/story/news/health/2020/12/23/high-risk-healthcare-workers-nch-healthcare-get-first-dose-covid-19-vaccine/4029190001/.

Allison Walters, who has worked at the NCH Downtown emergency room for two years, called it a "major development" to start getting the vaccine. A lot of patients with the virus are first screened in emergency rooms.

"It's just being in that environment and how closely we see everybody," Walters said. "It is very much a relief to come in and get that."

We quickly explained that NCH plans to be a local resource for the community to get vaccinated and will follow the state's plan that calls for high-risk healthcare workers, first responders, nursing home residents, and staff as a priority.

It's possible that people "sixty-five and older with health conditions can start getting vaccinated in the first quarter of next year," Dr. Lindner told the *Naples Daily News*.

Honestly, we had a huge emotional moment. You could hear a pin drop in the room. There were no words for this moment. You could see tears in the eyes of everyone in the room. Most of us could not even speak when the first employee received the vaccine. We had come full circle on our promise: a new covenant with the community. We had given all we had to fight this invader. Now we had access to the vaccine we needed to win the battle. It may have taken a while, but we got here. It's about winning.

It felt like a future without the nightmares.

CHAPTER 5

VICTORY OF HARMONY OVER DISCORD

Naples is all about water.

On the first anniversary of the arrival of the COVID-19 pandemic at NCH, a special memorial ceremony was held at the main entrance to NCH Naples Downtown. It was not insignificant that the tribute was a beautiful fountain.

Those who live in and visit Naples see fountains everywhere. It's a metaphor for the community. Since ancient times, a settlement's water source has been at the center of the community. From the well, the community drew water, the basic sustenance. Metaphorically, the fountain represents all the social resources of the community that are necessary for life, in a continuous flow, a powerful symbol of what a healthy and sustainable community looks like.

One year ago, the world changed. It hasn't been easy, but because of the healthcare heroes at NCH and around the world, we have persevered. Thank you to all healthcare professionals for the exceptional care and dedication throughout this pandemic and beyond.

—PAUL HILTZ · MARCH 11, 2021

We are also all about community, and the community donated the fountain. Last fall, when community members Rob and Cathy Funderburg learned about the opportunity to fund a new fountain as part of a beautification project at the downtown front entrance, they immediately said yes—with one stipulation: they wanted the fountain to be dedicated to healthcare professionals.

The community gathered for the unveiling. Our board of trustees and our physician leaders were here. This 830-pound granite fountain was crafted in Arizona. This recognition of the caregivers, the honors for those who were lost, and the flow of water symbolize everything good about the people who live here. A great community pauses to remember those who went before.

The Native Americans who stood on this soil, long before we did, believed that water has cleansing power. Water is a symbol for many things including life and death, strength, change, healing, dreaming, and unconditional love, all of which each of us has experienced in the past year. The Calusa Indians, who occupied this region as early as 1,450 BC, believed that each human had three souls present in their shadow, their reflection in water, and in the pupil of their eyes.[54]

---

54 Wikipedia, "Calusa," accessed March 15, 2024, https://en.wikipedia.org/wiki/Calusa#:~:text=The%20Calusa%20believed%20that%20the,and%20entered%20into%20an%20animal.

March 11, 2021

Excerpts of Opinion to the *Naples Daily News*

By Paul Hiltz, CEO of NCH Health System[55]

The sacrifices made by these professionals have been countless, and yet, they still come to work each day with a smile behind the mask, ready to care for the neighbors in their community. That spirit has gotten us through our hardships, and that spirit has been subsequently felt by the members who make up our vibrant Southwest Florida community.

I'd like to give many thanks to this community for their support, their encouragement, and their generous donations, not only to acknowledge our healthcare heroes but also to honor the many loved ones lost throughout the year to COVID-19. Together, we raised $1.89 million and received enough donations to purchase seven Xenex Germ-Zapping robots and five Advanced Ultra-Violet Systems UV Boxes, which will help to keep all our facilities consistently clean and sanitized.

Over the past year, more than 38,850 meals have been donated to NCH and our team. Throughout the long days and nights, this community made sure to care for those who care for us all with sustenance and sheer support; for that, I am so grateful.

---

55   Paul Hiltz, "Hope on the Horizon," *Naples Daily News*, March 11, 2021, accessed November 15, 0221, https://www.naplesnews.com/story/opinion/2021/03/11/one-year-anniversary-covid-19-we-have-hope-horizon-paul-hiltz/4611642001/.

"The courtyard will be a place of honor for our healthcare heroes who worked tirelessly on the front lines," NCH said in a statement to the press, "a place of respite for the loved ones of our patients, and a place of remembrance for the lives that were lost at NCH to COVID-19."

The *Naples Daily News* captured the emotional moments.

NCH director of spiritual care, Rev. Jennie Thomas, delivered a beautiful invocation and rang a bell 157 times—once for everyone who passed away from COVID-19 at NCH.

"When we were all in fear, they weren't concerned for themselves," said Naples mayor Teresa Heitmann of the healthcare workers.[56]

Dr. David Lindner and others working with him in the COVID-19 unit gathered to reflect on when the pandemic hit Naples.

"Suddenly this first patient was in the medical center with this disease," he recalled. Our healthcare workers did not understand whether this was something that we could be protected from or whether we could be lying in the bed next to them.

Paul Hiltz touched on the survivors. We are thankful for the "2,200 people discharged safely to their homes, and thousands more treated in the emergency department and released," Hiltz said. In the first year of the pandemic, NCH only had two exposures from a patient infecting a healthcare worker, and zero cases of patient-to-patient transmission.

Our organization had evolved through an existential disruption, followed by a horrible pandemic. The memories and emotions flowed through everyone's collective memories here that day. In essence, in

---

56 Liz Freeman, "NCH System Recognizes 'Healthcare Heroes' on the One-Year Anniversary of First COVID-19 Patient," *Naples Daily News*, March 11, 2021, accessed November 15, 2021, https://www.naplesnews.com/story/news/health/2021/03/11/nch-honors-health-care-workers-dedication-during-coronavirus-pandemic/6927113002/.

the past year we declared harmony over discord a victory. Then the immunization against a terrible virus.

What a long, strange trip it has been.

+ + +

Vaccinations began at the end of 2020 with healthcare workers and first responders, then those over sixty-five. On February 17, 2021, we began setting up to expand vaccinations to high-risk folks under sixty-five.

NCH worked with the state Department of Health to identify individuals sixty-five and younger who are at high risk and qualify. Then people with compromised immune systems were added to the eligibility. "Florida's Seniors First vaccine strategy is paying off," said Governor Ron DeSantis, "more than 3.2 million seniors sixty-five and older have received shots."[57]

The governor then expanded eligibility to those age fifty and above, and then to those age forty and above. On April 5, all adults in the state age eighteen and older became eligible for the vaccine. Governor DeSantis also reminded the public of the locations for immunizations with a press release on March 25.

"We've partnered with pharmacy retailers to offer the vaccine. There are now 1,600 pharmacies located throughout the state of Florida offering COVID-19 vaccines."

Paul Hiltz reflected about our journey.

---

57   Administration Schedule, "Governor Ron DeSantis Announces New Eligibility Guidelines for COVID-19 Vaccinations," March 25, 2021, accessed March 14, 2024, https://www.flgov.com/2021/03/25/governor-ron-desantis-announces-new-eligibility-guidelines-for-covid-19-vaccinations/#:~:text=Florida's%20Seniors%20First%20vaccine%20strategy,announce%20additional%20vaccine%20eligibility%20expansions.

LEADERSHIP TOOL KIT (PAUL)
SPIRITUAL LEADERSHIP

My church asked me to come in and give a talk on spiritual leadership. That's the topic, spiritual leadership in a secular healthcare organization. Leadership, itself, is a spiritual thing to me because you're trying to let people know that you're leading them to develop themselves as human beings and to be their highest and best self. You're trying to find a place for them to do that. The two things I've tried to listen and be a servant leader. I think listening, deep listening, is a spiritual thing. People in this world today don't feel like they're being listened to. They are not being heard. And the other thing is to be a servant leader; that's what Jesus, Gandhi, and Rev. Dr. Martin Luther King Jr. and all the great spiritual guides have tried to show us. They don't demand people to worship them. They, well, want people to *look at this example and follow me*. And that's what we're trying to do here. With the people I hire, I'm trying to get them to not be autocratic, serve other people, and serve the patients.

In early March, we announced a raise for employees and increased benefits. Our year-end financials were about break even. The big encouragement has been that through philanthropy, we received a total of $32 million, up from $18 million in 2018. Our "medical diplomats" program, in which supporters give $7,500 a year, has also rebounded, to more than seven hundred diplomats after dropping to around 460 two years ago.

Naples has always been a very generous community.

We purchased the Epic cloud-based EHR.

We acquired new offices by repurposing the *Naples Daily News* building, a victim of the downsizing in newspaper world. We have enhanced our NCH Heart Institute, pediatrics, and emergency facilities. We have again become a partner with the beloved Neighborhood Clinic. We've added new leadership. We've built highly effective teams. We have a new respect throughout the community for our mission.

What do you do when a crisis becomes commonplace? There was no break in the clouds in sight. What if this became the new norm indefinitely? We don't know, but it has gone on much longer than we could have anticipated.

Yet our brand has changed before our very eyes. And that sparked more conversations about the coming rebrand.

🛠 BRANDING TOOL KIT (AMANDA)
A BRAND CAN CHANGE IN MANY WAYS

How do we define rebranding? It can be much more than the traditional sense of a name change or a new logo, a new slogan or graphic look. Instead, for example, we have taken great care to channel our promotional energy into programs that can help save lives in the community ("All Heroes Wear Masks" with the City of Naples and "Southwest Florida Stronger Together" with Lee Health), not just about clinical advancements. As we reflect on the rebranding of NCH over the last year, the human interactions of listening and servant leadership have made great changes in our image and reputation. We have linked our reputation firmly to the world-class image of the Mayo Clinic. Lee Health joins us as a trusted partner in this struggle. The Neighborhood Clinic has welcomed us back. Other providers feel a part of a greater team with us. Clinically, we are still advancing despite the pandemic.

A few weeks before the fountain ceremony, Healthgrades announced their latest rankings. Southwest Florida hospitals were among the top 250 hospitals in the United States. According to the independent ranking firm, the two NCH hospitals earned recognition for quality and patient outcomes. That placed the hospitals in the top 5 percent of 4,500 hospitals nationwide that were evaluated based on clinical outcomes for thirty-two medical conditions and procedures.

We had restructured the management team. We launched a new emphasis on quality. Our once shattered "brand" was now emerging. We have reached out to become inclusive with the leadership of the region. Our physicians felt like they were being heard for the most part. Our donors regained confidence. Our employees felt like they were being listened to and protected. Doing the right thing well has been a powerful change agent. We continued our pursuit of long-range goals as summer arrived. Our physician recruitment efforts began to pay off as doctors from leading hospitals across the nation signed on.

Paul Hiltz noted that one of his favorite experiences at NCH has been recruiting a heart specialist to lead our heart institute.

"We have met a lot of smart people and their different approaches to leadership. And part of that, I went into the operating room with our new director, Dr. Robert Cubeddu, and watched him perform an advanced procedure. That was very, very enlightening."

The open-heart program has been here since 1996. In 2020, the NCH Heart Institute performed 441 open-heart procedures; total cardiac admissions were 3,375 for the fiscal year 2020.

"The NCH Heart Institute is expanding its cardiovascular services and hired a prominent cardiologist previously at Cleveland Clinic Florida, Robert Cubeddu, MD, to serve as president effective June 1." Dr. Cubeddu said NCH has built a strong foundation in its heart program that he will help grow.

"It's part of a strategy that NCH announced in April to transform its heart institute into a premier destination center for south Florida and beyond," we posted on our website.[58]

Robert Cubeddu, MD

"NCH is embracing clinical research opportunities and has already invested in clinical trials and research, many of which are underway," Dr. Cubeddu said in the interview. Dr. Cubeddu noted

---

58   NCH Heart Institute, https://nchmd.org/cardiology/cubeddu/, accessed March 14, 2024, https://nchmd.org/cardiology/cubeddu/.

that we utilize cutting-edge technology and innovation and in parallel we will encourage the implementation of physician-initiated trials through research grants and industry-sponsored trials.

On June 15, the new MitraClip procedure began at the NCH Heart Institute. The minimally invasive procedure repairs a leaky mitral valve to help restore normal blood flow through the heart. Left untreated, a mitral valve leak causes shortness of breath, fatigue, and other symptoms that diminish quality of life. Besides the MitraClip procedure, we added a new procedure approved by the FDA in February, intravascular lithotripsy, that uses sonic pressure waves to address hardened calcium deposits in the arteries so stents can be implanted to improve blood flow.

✦ ✦ ✦

Naples attracts some of the top leaders in the country. A lot of famous leaders live here, and we never tire of great interactions with these gifted people.

In early 2021, we looked back at what we learned while in the worst of the pandemic to review our strategies and evaluate whether to repeat those in the next pandemic. You see, our crystal ball said that this will not be the last such event. It was incumbent on us to document what went right. Fundamentally, the fact that we stayed true to quality and clinical development plans, aggressively communicated with media and community, partnered with the City of Naples and Lee Health to fight the pandemic, are all efforts we would repeat.

Matt Heinle, general counsel for NCH, noted that the new atmosphere of cooperation was welcome.

"There's definitely a higher degree of cooperation and the openness among all the different healthcare providers in our region than before the pandemic."

He observed that all the community's providers stepped up and did what they were built to do, and that's to take care of the community.

"At the same time, we are still competitors," Matt said, "but working together through a crisis and having that higher degree of cooperation, we've built a lot of bridges that were damaged in the past. It's a better situation, I think, a healthier situation, than before the pandemic."

On June 14, 2021, we announced another clinical advancement. The conversion of our EMR system to Epic had officially begun. Such a conversion affects nearly everyone at NCH. A team of dozens of Epic trainers arrived and began training every employee who uses medical records.

"The new Epic system puts patient care front and center," said Bryan Murphey, MD, ambulatory chief medical officer. It also allows NCH physicians to easily follow the medical care our patients may have received from their doctors elsewhere who also use the Epic system.

The Epic implementation allowed one chart to follow patients throughout the continuum of care at any NCH hospital, physician's office, or any other healthcare provider across the nation using Epic.

In May, we gave the news media tours of the new Simulation Center, which provides students and professionals with hands-on practice. WINK-TV News showed off the new state-of-the-art facility on May 11, 2021. The simulation gives a mockup of everything from a typical hospital room to the ER.[59]

---

59   Veronica Marshall, "Training Doctors and Nurses Using Real-World Simulations," WINK-TV News, May 11, 2021, accessed March 14, 2024, https://winknews.com/2021/05/11/training-doctors-and-nurses-using-real-world-simulations/.

"When Dr. Douglas Harrington, medical director of the Judith & Marvin Herb Family Simulation Center, was a resident at NCH, the jump from medical books to patients' bedsides was more of a leap," WINK-TV News reported.

"To do a procedure, I watched someone do it on a patient. The next time, I got to help. By the third time, I was doing it by myself," he said.

The center allows students and professionals to get realistic hands-on practice with mannequins who can cough, cry, and breathe.

"A study published by the National Institutes of Health finds that after practicing with simulations, one emergency department's detection of heart arrhythmia increased from five percent to 55 percent. Another healthcare system went from a 37 percent survival rate for cardiac arrest patients up to 42 percent," WINK-TV News reported.

We continued to march forward, and in June, we launched the upgrades to our birthplace and to our services for women and children over the next five years, so more families can receive care where they live.

+ + +

RESISTANCE

In mid-July 2021, things got tense again. The delta variant was now the dominant strain of the virus circulating in the state and Florida accounted for 20 percent of new infections nationwide.[60] According to state Department of Health data, the state reported 73,199 new infections, the single biggest surge since January 27. Florida now

---

60   Fenit Nirappil and Ashley Cusick, "When Delta Strikes: Latest Coronavirus Surges Grow Faster, Hit Record Heights in Louisiana, Florida," *Washington Post*, August 3, 2021, accessed March 14, 2024, https://www.washingtonpost.com/health/2021/08/03/covid-delta-surge-south/.

topped the list of super spreader states. Our hospitals filled up again, mostly with unvaccinated patients who were very ill. The *Washington Post* reported that while much of the country wrestled with masking guidance and new evidence of the dangers of the highly transmissible delta variant, public health authorities and doctors in the states hit hardest by the latest viral surge were confronting a new stage of the pandemic, unlike anything they have seen. That's us.

We struggled with COVID-19 as well as resistance to mask-wearing, confronting misinformation, and the weaponizing of fear. We must again urge people to lean on the science with us and under-stand what we see in the hospital. One of the rumors we dealt with people claiming that NCH houses illegal immigrants in the healthcare system, and that's why we see our COVID-19 numbers increasing …

For anyone who became symptomatic and was not vaccinated, we urged them to get treated with Regeneron. This infusion-based antibody cocktail must be administered within three days of the onset of symptoms to be most effective. Similarly, we preached the vital impor-tance for everyone to get vaccinated; the shots were freely available at NCH with an appointment and elsewhere in the community.

The *Washington Post* revealed that an infectious disease expert at Florida International University said new data from the CDC showed that the delta variant appeared to cause more severe illness and was transmissible by fully vaccinated people.[61]

"Delta spreads like wildfire. But vaccines contain that fire and will eventually help to put it out," said Dr. Aditi Nerurkar, a physician at Harvard Medical School. "For now, our shared goal must be to vaccinate everyone and avoid breeding vaccine discontentment.

---

61   Ibid.

Vaccines continue to be the surest bet to keep people out of hospitals, ICUs, and the obituary pages."[62]

"Unvaccinated Americans account for virtually all recent COVID-19 hospitalizations and deaths," said Jeff Zients, the White House COVID-19 response coordinator. "Each COVID-19 death is tragic, and those happening now are even more tragic because they are preventable."

Because people resisted the vaccine, we were having another, much worse, surge. On January 1, 2020, NCH employed thirty-five traveling nurses. When the delta variant hit in the summer, NCH filled 45 percent of the 190 nursing openings with traveling nurse staff. At the time, *it seemed like* this was the pandemic of the unvaccinated.[63]

It was here.

---

62 Ibid.

63 Becky Sullivan, "U.S. COVID Deaths Are Rising Again. Experts Call It a 'Pandemic of the Unvaccinated,'" NPR, July 16, 2021, accessed November 15, 2021, https://www.npr.org/2021/07/16/1017002907/u-s-covid-deaths-are-rising-again-experts-call-it-a-pandemic-of-the-unvaccinated.

CHAPTER 6

LISTEN. LEARN. LEAD.

On July 28, 2021, the *Fort Myers News-Press* reported that Lee Health experienced a 600 percent increase in COVID-19 hospitalizations over the last month.[64] NCH System experienced an 800 percent jump. These numbers were straining hospital resources, quickly nearing last summer's peaks. About 90 percent of the patients were unvaccinated, according to Lee Health. None of the vaccinated patients have needed treatment in an ICU. The average age of patients is fifty-eight, and two-thirds are under sixty-five. NCH treated ninety-five COVID-19 patients, up from twelve three weeks before. Of those, seventy-nine were unvaccinated.

The new surge of the more infectious delta variant attacked the unvaccinated around the country, and slowly but surely, the world. The war that was not going well was called "vaccination resistance."

---

64   Frank Gluck and Liz Freeman, "Lee Health COVID-19 Cases Up 600%, NCH Cases Up 800% as Southwest Florida Faces 'Pandemic of the Unvaccinated,'" Fort Myers News-Press, July 28, 2021, accessed November 1, 2021, https://www.news-press.com/story/news/2021/07/28/covid-19-hospitalizations-rise-lee-health-nch-health-care-system-delta-variant-unvaccinated/5405396001/.

The value proposition of accepting vaccination in exchange for longer life, the safety of loved ones, or the welfare of caregivers was met with a distrustful, frosty response. Our culture's escalating polarization was alive and well. Politicians kept telling us all what to do, not always based on science. Our doctors went on local television news. They pleaded with viewers who were choosing not to have a vaccination. They explained what was going on behind the walls of our hospitals.

DO YOU REALIZE WHAT IS HAPPENING HERE?

Midway into the second year of the struggle, vaccinations were making a huge difference for the vaccinated. But most of the desperately ill patients coming in the door now had no protection for themselves, their families, and their caregivers from the now-more-virulent delta variant COVID-19 because of their "personal freedom to choose."

While we invested our days masked up, seeking to win back the support and love of our community, we also tried to win the hearts and minds of people to vaccinate. We ramped up our partnership with the City of Naples and began discussions with them about a joint campaign to immunize the community. Few decisions at NCH are made without universal physician support, and the doctors were fully in favor of the campaign.

"They're coming for your freedoms."

Our clinical team still inhabited a dangerous bubble, trying to help their patients outlast the horror. Every moment of the day, for weeks, for months. Now this. Too many Collier County, Lee County, and Naples citizens still interpreted this choice as a fight for their freedom. The huge national debate about mandatory vaccinations found its way to Florida when NCH considered becoming one of the first hospital systems in our region of Florida to announce the employee mandate. Thankfully, we were not the first nationally. When we made the decision, over seventy-five healthcare organizations had already made the tough decision to require vaccination against COVID-19 to all employees, with only a few religious or other special exceptions.

Internally, not everyone was in alignment. Caregivers on the front lines and physicians in the ICU pushed hard for this vaccination policy. We began a serious, open dialogue internally about this, careful to be watchful of physician input.

Pitifully, this dreadnaught had become politicalized. The mandatory vaccination question could put at risk our recovering reputation and community trust. We believed that 99.9 percent of our doctors agreed with the mandate. You're always going to have exceptions. A few physicians pushed back because of their belief system. They got the vaccine themselves. They said enabling the vaccine was the right thing, but some questioned making it mandatory for all employees. Some felt like there was still not enough data and science. However, all our physicians acknowledged that we know what COVID-19 does. We know what happens if you don't get the vaccine. Just take a walk with us through our hospitals.

We had ten people under age forty die in one August week. We knew that unvaccinated people were flooding our healthcare system, and it was just going to get worse. Sure, there could be risks and consequences, but we knew what outweighed the risks here—the safety of our staff and patients. Most everyone was on board. But among the most resistant, and this troubled us, were young nurses who expressed concern about fertility issues. We addressed this head-on, and tried to meet with all the nurses of childbearing age to alleviate their concerns. We published a testimonial, which was helpful to many young employees.

"As a critical care nurse during the outbreak and seeing what COVID-19 does and can do to healthy people, I am 100 percent for the vaccine," said Ellison Van Cleef Warner RN, BSN, director of physician relations at NCH.

"It was a personal decision, one that was not easy to make, especially while I was pregnant. However, I discussed it thoroughly with my OB-GYN and my husband. We spent weeks researching and discussing the science behind the mRNA vaccine. When weighing the options, we believed that there were more severe risks to myself and the baby if I were to get COVID-19 during my pregnancy," Ellison Van Cleef Warner, RN, wrote.

"I did wait to get the vaccine once I was in the second trimester, and I did not have any reactions. I had a wonderful, healthy, and full-term pregnancy and today, both baby and I are great! I'm confident in my personal choice and happy I got the Moderna vaccine to protect myself and others. I would love to know if my antibodies crossed, and that my healthy newborn is protected as well!"

I am not being disrespectful.
I'm trying to save their life.

Paul Hiltz shared an anecdote with his staff from these troublesome days.

"Dr. Harrington took me out of my office and upstairs to a COVID unit and said, 'watch this.' We stood outside a room with a COVID-19 patient on an ECMO, a heart-lung machine."

He said, "'Stand here for a minute, because that alarm's going to start going off. And then people are going to run into that room.'"

It did not take long. We stood there looking in.

"And their mask might, or might not, be on at all," Dr. Harrington said, "it might be on improperly. But their instincts will take over. And they will run in, and if they're not vaccinated, they're going to end up critically ill themselves."

That experience weighed heavily on our decision. Our instinct was to protect the staff because it made sense.

That's why it hurts your feelings when people say, well, *you're being disrespectful to your own staff.* It's a slap in the face.

"I am not being disrespectful. I'm trying to save their life," Paul recalled.

We made a tough decision. The board, medical executive committee, and management team agreed unanimously. The decision was announced, along with a September 16, 2021, deadline for all employees to be vaccinated.

The decision and the press release occurred just hours apart. There is no time for discussion, no time for venting opposition, and a huge opportunity to say, Here they go again ...

The leadership team rolled it out within twenty-four hours, with unblinking assurance that we had no time for messy democracy about this, of all things. This was about the safety of our staff and patients. We feared that it would be leaked, and things would get out before we could proactively get the announcement to the media. The decision occurred at about 7:00 a.m. and was announced to physicians at 8:00 a.m. Employees were notified right after that. The press came by at 10:00 a.m.

In this case, almost all NCH physicians pushed for the rapid decision. But not every one of them. It always has been our instinct to lead, not follow. Our notion was to maintain transparency, and any delay in announcement could be criticized by a news media that usually responds to a call that said, You will not believe what is happening at NCH.... We felt compelled to announce quickly. We knew that someone in the building would have called the newspaper or TV five minutes after we made the decision.

Some physicians disagreed with the decision, noting that we don't all align on the science yet. There was still a lot of discourse. The science was constantly changing, and the variants were evolving. New journals came out every day. So even within the scientific community and physician community, not everyone agreed on everything.

Citizens organized a protest and rally against it because they thought it was against civil rights and liberties to make people do this as a condition of employment. Even though they may have agreed with the vaccine, they did not agree with it being a condition of employment in the healthcare system. We braced for the coming rally.

"This was a bitter pill to swallow for many of us," noted Dr. Carlos Quintero.

"We felt the vaccines were going to help. The majority of those infected now came in unvaccinated."

Dr. Quintero recalled that some doctors did not like the mandate. Eventually, the medical staff leadership decided that we would make it a mandate for physicians and providers coming through to be vaccinated unless they had a valid excuse, either religious or medical. Then we formed a physician-led task force to review the exceptions.

"This was most challenging," Dr. Quintero noted.

Gregory Poland, MD, director of Mayo Clinic's Vaccine Research Group, supported NCH's new policy with a powerful statement.

"For us as physicians, we take a pledge to protect and preserve the health of those who trust themselves to our care, and for that reason we require a variety of immunizations from our healthcare providers," said Dr. Poland.

"The COVID vaccine is simply the latest vaccine required to protect the health of our patients and of the public. It is a duty we dare not shrink away from and the science is clear. The most important thing you can do to protect your health and well-being, that of your family, and that of your community is to get a vaccine. I support NCH and their commitment to keep their staff and community safe."

You have to follow the science
when the world is on fire.

Dr. Poland served on our academic staff here as an adjunct professor with the NCH Mayo Clinic Care Network.

Jonathan Kling, RN, recalled that in the beginning of the pandemic and throughout, "Dr. Poland, Dr. Linder, and I had many conversations. In fact, my very first town hall *WebEx* for our staff, Dr. Poland was on it with me, and Dr. Linder. When we started talking about mandatory vaccinations, it was pretty intense at the very beginning. Dr. Gregory Poland calmed everyone."

"I'm up here at Mayo. You're seeing it across the United States. You're seeing it across the world. Colleges and universities are requiring it. Private employers and other business sectors are doing it because you have to follow the science when the world is on fire like this, and you cannot overcome all the misconceptions that people have."

As the NCH board decision settled, approximately 1,500 employees were not vaccinated. Our deadline for vaccination was September 16. Once we considered the possible consequences, we could face the discharge of hundreds of great nurses and more support personnel.

The day that happens, it will feel like rounding third base, and home plate will look like a hole in the ground.

As storytellers, we can look down from the ceiling on such a scene and imagine the possibilities if we do not stand by our muscular statement. Should we reconsider? This felt like "Catch-22," a dilemma defined in Joseph Heller's 1961 satirical war novel of that name, later a hit movie, from which there is no escape because of mutually conflicting or dependent conditions. After we all commit to this mandatory policy, we will have another crisis on our hands. If we rescind the policy, we would be failing our patients and staff. We could lose all credibility. The only answer was to convince our employee population to get vaccinated before the deadline. Basketball fans will understand. We needed a "full court press."

On Sunday, August 1, WINK-TV News covered the protest rally.

"Demonstrators covered all four corners of the intersection at Immokalee Road and Health Care Boulevard, which is right outside of NCH North."[65]

WINK-TV News reported that the local healthcare system has become one of the first hospitals in Florida to require employees to get the COVID-19 vaccine. Protesters came with signs and flags and were chanting in opposition to the vaccine mandate. One of the protesters said, "It's a first amendment right. They have a right to decide. Our bodies, our choice."

WINK-TV News reported that all leaders, physicians, providers, contract staff, and volunteers were required to be fully vaccinated as a condition of employment. More than a week before, the hospital system said it was requiring that new hires be vaccinated, "but with

---

65 "Dozens Protest NCH Vaccination Mandate," WINK-TV News, August 1, 2021, accessed November 15, 2021, https://www.winknews.com/2021/08/01/dozens-protest-nch-vaccination-mandate/.

the latest surge due to the delta variant, the hospitals announced the change Friday."

Fox 4 TV included in their report that "several NCH employees have reached out to me this week, because NCH has changed their policy … and they're upset because they don't want to take the vaccine, but they don't wish to lose their jobs. So, NCH is putting them in a very tough spot."[66] We put up a stoic front during the protests.

It was frustrating that there was such a controversy around this vaccine for healthcare workers. We didn't think the federal government should mandate it, either. But we did feel a private business, especially one in healthcare, ought to be able to require it.

> The NCH Medical Executive Committee unanimously endorsed NCH's new vaccination policy on Friday. NCH leads the region in implementing this policy to take steps to safeguard the health and well-being of our staff and patients further. The new COVID variants are much more transmittable and at least five times more contagious than previous ones. Over 90 percent of COVID-19 inpatients are unvaccinated, and 100 percent of ICU patients are unvaccinated. We are seeing younger people sicker, and this has become an unvaccinated pandemic.

While NCH was a leader in Southwest Florida with this decision, joined by large employers outside of healthcare like Google, Publix, and Disney, we were gratified that the Mayo Clinic required all employees to be vaccinated by September 17, 2021. We appeared on

---

66 Fox 4 News at 10, August 1, 2021, accessed November 15, 2021, https://www.youtube.com/watch?v=dpGhQF5c4SA.

the NBC Nightly News, CBS, and the Today Show. This occurred during a dramatic surge requiring us to activate our surge plans fully. We brought in dozens of traveling nurses. We brought in locum tenens traveling physicians to help. We did not need this distraction. Paul Hiltz was becoming a bit stern with his public appearances.

"We need to unify more than ever," he noted during the television update on the increasing number of COVID-19 cases and our plans to respond to the rise in hospitalizations.

The protesters were still beating the drum a week after the Sunday protest.[67] One of our community's most beloved physicians had enough. He got everyone's attention. On August 9, 2021, NBC2 News aired one of the most emotional moments of the pandemic with a powerful interview. NBC2 News interviewed NCH critical care physician Dr. Douglas Harrington, who was very upset.[68]

Dr. Harrington struggled not to break down emotionally. He was tired. He was sad. He was angry. Every bone in his body was screaming that this should not be. Circumstances caught up with Dr. Harrington on this ninth day of August after eighteen months of battling the dragon.

We are having people die, and it is getting harder ...
to come to work every day ... when this was
preventable.

—DOUG HARRINGTON, MD

---

67   Ibid.

68   "Doctors Make Emotional Plea," NBC2 News, August 9, 2021, accessed November 15, 2021, https://nbc-2.com/news/local/2021/08/06/ nch-doctors-make-emotional-plea-as-covid-19-tightens-grip-on-younger-people/.

Dr. Harrington said the delta variant is five times more contagious than the alpha. Just one person can easily infect nine people.

"Previously, we saw older individuals with past medical problems," he said.

"It took those patients one to two weeks to become critically ill."

"We have a team of nine critical care doctors, led by pulmonologist Dr. Vishal Patel and Dr. David Lindner. We will work seven days in a row, 120 hours in those seven days, and we spend the entire time in the ICU, and it's very challenging and stressful for the medical team. Last year, we knew what was coming. We were prepared. Now, within hours, one person can infect multiple people. *(Snaps his fingers)* Like that."

Dr. Harrington added that we are now literally converting non-ICU beds into ICUs. "If the room has a door and we can put negative pressure in, we'll convert it. We have plenty of respirators, plenty of personnel."

"But the thing I am absolutely scared about is if the team can continue to stand together and fight endlessly. We … are right at the top."

"We're now seeing all the way from two years old up to one hundred years old in this hospital."

Most patients now seen in NCH hospitals with COVID-19 are younger and healthy. They're becoming critical not in a week or two but within days, "so that ability to see the patient, to have days to get them on treatment, is not in our hands anymore," he added.

"Now, they come in the hospital, and within twenty-four hours, they're in the ICU."

"People are dying. The time is now. We need to come together as a community and vaccinate."

"We all had those moments during the delta phase. It was pretty tough, but we pulled through together," COVID-19 Task Force cochair Jonathan Kling, RN, said.

The latest reported numbers showed fifty-eight people died every day on average from COVID-19 in Florida—the highest average in the nation.

So far, no one had resigned because of the new policy at NCH, with staff vaccination at 70 percent. As of August 6, 153 patients were seeking help in NCH hospitals for COVID-19, 90 percent unvaccinated. That was an all-time high for the institution. Thirty-six of the 153 are in the ICU, an increase of ten patients twenty-four hours prior. Of the thirty-six, 94 percent were unvaccinated.

Mariann MacDonald made an observation several years after these protests that rings so true:

> We knew we were doing the right thing for the patients and the community, and yet we had all this pushback. You had non-maskers and anti-vaxxers, and you just knew you were right, and here come the rallies. I hope people understand that these things can happen even when someone like Amanda is guiding the communications. But if you do not have organized communications, and these events strike home, you are in real trouble, like the hospitalist crisis. It's vital: how you communicate, how you market, how you listen, and how you build that trust. That's how Amanda and Paul plowed through the madness so quickly. They showed the community that they were listening and kept saying that they would always do the right thing for our patients and staff.

⚒ PR TOOL KIT (AMANDA)
STAYING SHARP

Even trained spokespersons can be caught flat-footed when the world is on fire. Another news media issue during this second surge was that the devoted spokespersons were tired. When we worked with key physicians and executives to become the voice of NCH, we should have accounted for the fact that they might be exhausted when we asked them to interview. In Dr. Harrington's case, his exhaustion was an asset to the interview. Somebody had to get vulnerable to get the attention of the public. Everyone's getting worn out. Staying on message takes work. It takes focus. "Brevity is the soul of wit" (Shakespeare from *Hamlet*).[69] Simply put, brevity is the soul of wit means that alert, clever people can express intelligent things using very few words. (Key word *alert*.)

A good example of this occurred when Dr. David Lindner testified in Tallahassee about COVID-19. Dr. Lindner listened carefully to our last-minute coaching. He nailed the interview perfectly. He was concise. He stayed on message. He didn't criticize any politicians. He smiled. His victory carried over to other media opportunities. If your spokesperson wants to be on camera, the camera reveals that to the viewers, who feel that this person *wants* to be speaking to me. Dr. Lindner became one of the most trusted physicians in the region.

---

69   Shakespeare, *MacBeth*, 4.3 Act 4 Scene 1, 10–11, Play Shakespeare.com, accessed March 11, 2024, https://www.playshakespeare.com/macbeth/scenes/248-act-iv-scene-1.

Our constant use of our physicians as spokespersons, either for the health system or for their service line, had a few drawbacks. Extremely busy physicians at the heart of the pandemic would do Zoom interviews from their offices. Or from their car. We created a "pop-up" display and recording equipment so the physician could push a button and record their message. Our backgrounds were always professional, and the doctors liked the ease of doing it.

+ + +

As the pandemic of the unvaccinated surged through NCH, we got back with the City of Naples and again put forth a public campaign designed to help save lives. The *CommUNITY ImmUNITY* campaign with the City of Naples encouraged citizens to vaccinate. We also launched a new website NaplesInUnity.com, to provide insight on community COVID-19 numbers and provide data from their hospitals. City Council urged residents to wear masks and get vaccinated. Our NCH management team also fanned out into the community with the campaign.

Luckily, on August 23, 2021, the US FDA approved the first COVID-19 vaccine. (The vaccines had previously been available with an EUA.)[70]

This long-awaited decision gave us some room to adjust our mandate deadline at least. Acting FDA commissioner Dr. Janet Woodcock observed that "while millions of people have already safely received COVID-19 vaccines, we recognize that for some, the FDA approval of a vaccine may now instill additional confidence to get vaccinated. Today's milestone puts us one step closer to altering the course of this pandemic in the United States."[71]

The vaccine also continued to be available under EUA, including for individuals twelve through fifteen years of age and for the administration of a third dose in certain immunocompromised individuals.

Room to breathe. Our mobile field hospital system was standing by. While the vocal protesters would continue their protest, the FDA had thrown us a life preserver, rendering moot one of the major objections to immunization. At the end of August, we had 71 percent more infected patients than the month before. Other regional hospitals also struggled. Florida became the new epicenter of the pandemic.

By September 1, 2021, 82 percent of the 209 COVID-19 patients at NCH System were unvaccinated people. They were very sick. On this day, NCH operated at 130 percent of its staffed critical care bed capacity, with sixty-one ICU beds occupied. During the first wave of the pandemic, NCH's highest COVID-19 patient count was 144, set on July 15, 2020.

As the deadline for staff vaccinations got closer, many employees who watched Dr. Harrington's television interview got the vaccine.

---

70   FDA, US Food and Drug, "FDA Approves First Covid-19 Vaccine," August 23, 2021, accessed November 3, 2021, https://www.fda.gov/news-events/press-announcements/fda-approves-first-covid-19-vaccine.

71   Will Brothers, "A Timeline of COVID-19 Vaccine Development."

The final confirmed approval of the Pfizer vaccine helped those who were waiting for that moment. Our management team met with every employee who was delinquent on vaccinations. NCH also announced a monetary incentive for getting fully vaccinated.

"We wanted to do everything to encourage our team members to get vaccinated. We put in that financial incentive, and then, I believe some team members thought maybe we would change our mind and not mandate," General Counsel Matt Heinle recalled.

"Literally, the last week before the mandate went into effect, many team members got the one-shot vaccine. It was coming down to the wire, and even after the deadline passed, a few employees came in with their vaccine card because they realized that we were serious and were mandating the vaccine," he said.

That was helpful. By the September 16, 2021, deadline, we had reached 99 percent vaccination. We only had to set free about one hundred who refused vaccination. And we have hired one hundred new caregivers who protect their patients with immunizations.

It was a big day when NCH achieved 99 percent fully vaccinated employees.

The countdown during the last four weeks was intense.

"Every hour of the day was spent on vaccinations, who had what, logging it into the system, doing statistics, processing the exemptions."

Renee Thigpen explained that there were two groups evaluating exemptions: a group processing religious exemptions and a group of providers looking at the medical exemptions.

All employee identifiers were redacted to protect privacy and comply with HIPAA (Health Insurance Portability and Accountability Act of 1996), a federal law that required the creation of national standards to protect sensitive patient health information from being disclosed without the patient's consent or knowledge.[72]

"So, we gave each applicant a number and got them into the system. There were many moving parts. I probably said this a million times; it was like herding minnows," Renee Thigpen said.

"Herding minnows was all I could think of because it was moving so fast, and leaders were calling and saying, 'Well, why didn't you approve this?'"

They would not breach confidentiality.

"We were the policy police. All we were trying to do is treat people fairly. We collectively, as an organization, made decisions, and we helped facilitate that."

She said they did not accept anybody being ugly about it. Renee told her HR staff to remember that "at the end of the day, you're doing the right thing and it's not you. It's the process, the new rule, that they're upset with, but they're taking it out on you. But it is not you."

NCH was taken to task by a few employees who were approved for being unvaccinated but objected to having a coded indicator on their employee badge. The hospitals needed to have a mechanism to understand who should be masking and testing. The controversy did not last long.

NCH changed the logo location on the badge to serve as a visible but subtle vaccination status. We felt like the past two months had been the most difficult of the pandemic. The physicians kept saying it was preventable now. We all knew this should not be happening. We could prevent it. When they come in, they are hanging onto life. Healthcare workers on the front lines were dealing with this, and it is extraordinarily hard to watch. This has taken a toll.

---

72 CDC, "Health Insurance Portability and Accountability Act of 1996 (HIPAA)," accessed March 9, 2024, https://www.cdc.gov/phlp/publications/topic/hipaa.html.

It was difficult to go to work during this phase of the pandemic because all this effort was unnecessary. Our fire and rescue first responders know this feeling. So do soldiers being sent to fight a war that few care about. To quote BB King, "The thrill is gone."[73]

Yet, COVID-19 had another variant to test us. The Omicron variant emerged.

On March 7, 2023, American Medical Association (AMA) news editor Sara Berg, MS, published a retrospective article on the AMA website entitled "Why COVID-19 deaths among vaccinated show that boosters matter."[74]

"The bivalent COVID-19 vaccine booster—which was first recommended last fall—protected against infection and death during the circulation of BA.4 and BA.5 Omicron subvariants. In fact, people who received the updated COVID-19 bivalent booster were fourteen times less likely to die compared with those who received no vaccine. They were also three times less likely to die compared with those who received only the primary series of COVID-19 vaccines, according to a report from the CDC."[75]

It was still bad all over the world.

The WHO noted that "on 30 January 2020 COVID-19 was declared a Public Health Emergency of International Concern (PHEIC) with an official death toll of 171. By 31 December 2020, this figure stood at 1,813,188. Yet preliminary estimates suggest the total number of global deaths attributable to the COVID-19 pandemic in

---

73   Genius, B.B. King, accessed March 14, 2024, https://genius.com/
      Bb-king-the-thrill-is-gone-lyrics.

74   Sara Berg, "Why COVID-19 Deaths among Vaccinated Show That Boosters Matter,"
      AMA, accessed March 11, 2024, https://www.ama-assn.org/delivering-care/
      public-health/why-covid-19-deaths-among-vaccinated-show-boosters-matter.

75   Ibid.

2020 is at least three million, representing 1.2 million more deaths than officially reported."[76]

The Most Terrifying Moment of the Pandemic

By chief nursing officer Jonathan Kling, RN
Cochair, NCH COVID-19 Task Force

During the delta variant surge, we had 240 patients in our health-care system that were COVID-19 positive, about 50 percent of our patients.

This was the peak moment of the pandemic, and the oxygen demand was rising fast.

Healthcare systems like ours use liquid oxygen to supply our patients. Every COVID-19 patient was on 100 percent oxygen.

We have big liquid oxygen tanks that hold about three hundred inches of liquid oxygen.

And on a usual day with the census of five hundred patients, we would use about an inch and a half of liquid oxygen. But deep in this surge, we were using about sixteen to twenty inches a day of liquid O2.

There was more bad news. When you run your air very cold at home, sometimes your lines can freeze, even if it's a hundred degrees outside. Pressures for oxygen were dropping and, the patients weren't getting the O2 they needed. We had to emer-

---

76   World Health Organization, Health Topics, "The True Death Toll of COVID-19," 2021, accessed March 12, 2024, https://www.who.int/data/stories/the-true-death-toll-of-covid-19-estimating-global-excess-mortality.

gently bring hot water and have sprinklers on our pipes, so they would never freeze. This had never happened before. And then the supply chain team reported that there's a national shortage and only two places in the nation have an available supply, in South Carolina and Texas. And of course, they couldn't hire truck drivers. So, what's next?

I was thinking, *Oh my God, we have 240 patients. If we run out of oxygen, what are we going to do?* This could be catastrophic. How much O2 do we have in the tanks and how do we triage who's more important to get the oxygen over who, right? Those are ethical decisions and crises that made my knees shake.

Every hospital in the state was in a similar situation. We called the Department of Health. We called the governor. We called senators. All agencies were rationing their supplies at every level, and the best we could arrange was delivery of about twenty inches every other day. We needed twice that, and it was getting worse.[77]

Tense days passed. We were just hours away from running out of oxygen every day. National news reported that the shortage was worst in Florida where, according to a survey conducted by the Florida Hospital Association, sixty-eight Florida hospitals had less than two days of oxygen available. And since the

---

77   Advisory Board, Daily Briefing, "The Latest Pandemic Shortage: Oxygen," September 1, 2021, accessed May 1, 2022, https://www.advisory.com/daily-briefing/2021/09/01/oxygen-shortage.

beginning of July, twenty-nine hospitals have had their oxygen supplies drop below twelve hours.[78]

More than seventeen thousand patients were currently hospitalized with COVID-19 in Florida, *WUSF Public Media* reported. And according to data from federal health officials and Johns Hopkins University, the state reported the highest COVID-19 hospitalization rate in the country at seventy-five patients per one hundred thousand residents. But our decision to not get in the way, to delegate responsibility, to let the people on the front lines make the decisions, paid off. My team told me to relax.

Jon, we're talking to the right people. We'll make this work. We have a plan. Trust that we're doing this right.

I was still scared. *Well ... tell me what you're doing.*

Our team was empowered to do whatever they thought was best, and we made it through.

They planned to acquire smaller external tanks. They were able to secure a couple thousand portable tanks.

But the amount of money we had to spend to do it was ... crazy. However, they knew that I wasn't going to give them grief for spending money to take care of our patients. And neither was our board, and neither would Paul, because it was the right thing to do.

---

78   Abe Aboraya, "FHA Survey: 68 Florida Hospitals Have Less Than 48 Hours' Worth of Oxygen," Health News Florida, August 26, 2021, accessed March 14, 2024, https://health.wusf.usf.edu/health-news-florida/2021-08-26/fha-survey-68-florida-hospitals-have-less-than-48-hours-worth-of-oxygen.

But that was probably for me the most terrifying time because, you don't have control, right? We had a real fear that we might not be successful. But we were, because our team was empowered to lead, to be creative, and to make decisions without fear.

+ + +

We commissioned the organizational consultant Korn Ferry to come to NCH and perform an audit, do focus groups, and start talking with the healthcare team about "How do we fix the culture here?"

What do we need to do from a human resources perspective? The results were disappointing. And while we believe that we have made big progress at the top level of the organization, it must happen at every level throughout the organization.

🔧 BRANDING TOOL KIT (AMANDA)
A BRAND IS YOUR VOICE

Oftentimes, management finds themselves with significant challenges in the process of being deliberate about the company brand. In many cases, there will be many stakeholders who care deeply about the corporate identity and image. Still, they do not have any experience with it or a marketing and communications background.

They haven't gone through a rebranding before, and when many folks hear about rebranding, they immediately start suggesting a new logo. That's where it stops. New logo. New brand.

So, education plays a big role in preparing your stakeholders for the process ahead. A brand is your voice, how you show up in the market, and how people talk about you. It's your tone, what you look like, and so many other things.

We first need to learn to talk about ourselves differently. All our messaging must change. We closely plan the hierarchy of communication (what we say about ourselves, and to whom) and we make sure we are very deliberate about communicating in a seamless cascade of messaging, so everyone feels included and not left behind.

The value proposition has changed.

When an organization begins to reshape the branding of the company, usually the value proposition has changed. You are not what you once were. Things have happened fast, which redefines you. For instance, our physician leadership shies away from using the name "community" healthcare, as that moniker implies small local organization rather than major regional referral center on the leading edge of medicine. But with our donors, the word community indicates a strong community voice, "our" hospital, and communicates belonging.

In advancing the reputation and brand for our NCH Rooney Heart Institute, we initially began discussions on the overall "brand" of the NCH System. We had not been in a big rush to address this, but despite the pandemic we advanced new ideas on rebranding our heart center. Big ideas begin to percolate. In August, we did another survey, this time of our physicians. This was a comprehensive Press Ganey survey, one of the top healthcare consultants in the country.

We were generally pleased with rising confidence in the leadership, except in two areas. Our doctors still rated NCH with low scores in response to the question: "I have adequate input into determining the leadership of the hospital."

That hurt, but again, when we recalled what our medical staff had been through with the disruption, the pandemic, and staff shortages, we probably should have expected that.

One of the things we heard from physicians, and this was affecting the scores, was not having enough staff. We were still short-staffed. We couldn't get enough people, and at times we were struggling. Doctors were, rightfully, holding the administration accountable for that as well. *Why haven't we filled these positions?* We had a crisis of talent in every industry in the whole country. This was not unique to healthcare. Certainly, healthcare probably felt it the worst. We were seeing critical numbers of professionals exiting healthcare altogether. We didn't have enough nurses. The only remedy was traveling nurses and the increased cost of that impacting the morale of full-time staff. One thing that has not hurt NCH is that Naples has been again rated one of the best places to live in America by several surveys.

"It may be getting more expensive to live, but Southwest Florida remains at the top of the 'Best Places to Retire' in the country, based on the latest *U.S. News & World Report* research," the *Naples Daily News* reported.[79]

"The state's metros led the way, with the first four in this order: Sarasota, Naples, Daytona Beach, and Melbourne.

---

79   Phil Fernandez, "In the Know: Forget Arizona and Texas. Sarasota, Naples, Daytona, Melbourne Are 'Best Places to Retire,'" *Naples Daily News*, October 19, 2021, accessed March 4, 2024, https://www. naplesnews.com/story/news/columnists/in-the-know/2021/10/19/ sarasota-naples-daytona-melbourne-best-places-retire/8455971002/.

"Many retirees are continuing to dream about a Florida beach retirement," said Emily Brandon, *U.S. News & World Report* senior editor for retirement. "Sarasota and Naples residents both report a high sense of well-being, and both cities scored high marks for desirability. Sarasota edged out Naples for the Number one spot largely due to Sarasota having more affordable housing than Naples."

As the year 2021 marched past, the pandemic leveled out. Admissions eased, but our immunization campaign continued. Our physicians believed we have begun to experience some herd immunity. As the year drew to a close, we looked back. We immunized our population, rolled out two beautiful public health campaigns, faced down a vaccination protest, and advanced clinically in every area. We were not out of the woods yet. The pandemic still lurked.

But two pieces of very good news arrived. The first big headline in the *Naples Daily News*: "Healthgrades releases specialty hospital awards: As NCH plans new heart institute, cardiac care recognized again."

"The NCH System in Collier County is one of the nation's 100 Best Hospitals in Cardiac Care, according to new ratings by Healthgrades. It is the seventh year in a row that the hospital's cardiac program has been recognized," the newspaper reported.[80]

Healthgrades evaluates nearly 4,500 hospitals nationwide across thirty-one common procedures and conditions. It used Medicare patient data from 2018 to 2020. Cardiac patients treated at any of Healthgrades' *100 Best Hospitals for Cardiac Care* have, on average, a 27.8 percent lower mortality risk than if they were treated at a hospital that did not receive the award, the *Naples Daily News* reported.

---

80 Liz Freeman, "Healthgrades Releases Specialty Hospital Awards: As NCH Plans New Heart Institute, Cardiac Care Recognized Again," November 9, 2021, *Naples Daily News*, accessed March 14, 2024, https://www.naplesnews.com/story/news/health/2021/11/09/healthgrades-recognizes-cardiac-care-nch-healthcare-system-7th-year-row/6336426001/.

"At the NCH Heart Institute, we are transforming cardiac care," Robert Cubeddu, MD, president of the Heart Institute, said in a news release. "We're not only committed to providing our patients with clinical excellence, but we're also committed to strengthening our foundation in research, education, and innovation." Dr. Cubeddu provides an inside look at the NCH Heart Institute in a powerful, inspiring television commercial we produced, appearing late in 2021.

The *Naples Daily News* also described our plans for a $150 million freestanding NHC Heart Institute adjacent to NCH Baker Downtown to expand services and address growth in the region.

"This will be an investment by NCH (estimated) to be $150 million that will support a state-of-the-art facility in the city of Naples and elevate the reputation of our community with the goal of becoming a destination for world-class healthcare," we said in a letter to the Naples Mayor and the city council, which after considerable study approved the project in 2024.

NCH performs about 450 cardiac bypass surgeries annually. The awards recognized superior clinical performance in seventeen specialty areas and included a new category for overall surgical care. Healthgrades also recognized NCH for clinical achievement in stroke care for the fourth year in a row, and for pulmonary care, gastrointestinal care, and critical care for three years in a row. NCH was recognized for gastrointestinal surgery two years in a row.

The second piece of good news occurred on November 9, when WINK-TV News aired a story about honoree Paul Hiltz leading a team during the pandemic.

Gulfshore Life magazine had just recognized him as one of their eight "men and women of the year," an award that is given to a select few culinary, design, art, and civic innovators who are enriching the cultural fabric of Southwest Florida, it was reported.

In the news report, the article noted that "running a hospital never ends for Hiltz, even as the pandemic slows. In fact, now is when the real work starts," he said. Paul Hiltz noted in the interview that "the ER has been expanded and will now be almost fifty thousand square feet at NCH Baker, with more private rooms and new technologies built in," WINK-TV News reported.[81] Now, the hospital's laser-focused on the new heart institute.

"Cardiovascular disease is still the number one killer in America," said Hiltz. The building is a work in progress, but the medical profession has already started.

"We've got fifteen clinical trials going on in cardiac disease. We're expanding our residency program; we'll have forty-eight internal medicine residents in conjunction with Mayo Clinic."

As Hiltz looks toward the future, he'd be remiss not to recognize all the doctors, nurses, and volunteers who kept the hospital running during a pandemic.

"It's people putting the patient first and putting the patient in front of everything else."

---

81   Lindsay Sablan, "NCH CEO Shares His Vision for the Future of the Hospital," WINK-TV News, November 9, 2021, accessed November 15, 2021, https://www. winknews.com/2021/11/09/nch-ceo-shares-his-vison-for-the-future-of-the-hospital/.

PART 4

—

HIGH CHEESE

CHAPTER 7

LOOKING PAST THE CRISIS

On March 17, 2020, this headline appeared in the *New York Times* in an article regarding the role of face masks in times of the COVID-19 outbreak:

The surgical face mask
has become a symbol of our times.[82]

From our perspective, *heroism* has become a symbol of our times. They just happened to be wearing masks. All heroes wear masks. We have seen so many heroes. Perhaps the *New York Times* paid homage to that fact. These heroes are unheralded personally, but as a group, as a societal force, they have made their mark on our times.

---

82 Vanessa Freidman, "The Mask," March 17, 2020, *New York Times*, accessed November 1, 2021, https://www.nytimes.com/2020/03/17/style/face-mask-coronavirus.html.

SACRIFICE AND SATISFACTION

Jonathan Kling, RN, stood at the center of the fire. He joined NCH in 2003 as a bedside nurse and in surgical ICU. He served as chief nursing officer through the pandemic, chairing the NCH COVID-19 Task Force. Now chief operating officer for NCH, Jon recalled the personal impact of the management crisis and pandemic. He characterized his journey as rewarding, exhausting, punctuated by guilt and happiness, followed by guilt.

"And I'll tell you why I say guilt twice. Because at the beginning, the genesis of the leadership transition from our previous CEO to Paul, I felt like I didn't do enough to maybe lead the strategy in a different direction. And then I felt guilty that our nursing staff had to go through the public relations nightmare they did, because all they were trying to do was help our community and take care of them.

"And then I felt guilty because I wasn't spending time with my family, or I'd feel guilty because I was going home, and I felt like I should still be at work. Or I felt guilty about having my phone during my kids' story time before bed.

"I said guilt one last time because I'm so passionate about our organization, our community, and our staff that I felt guilty that I was leaving, and I felt guilty that I was home. It's been a challenge to that work-life balance. I have been learning to be better with all this.

"I felt rewarded because we were able to keep the staff engaged in what they do best (and that's patient care) and keeping patients and family at the center of all they do. We made it through that, and then it was rewarding to repair relationships and listen and learn from 'the sins and mistakes of our fathers and mothers,' to steal a phrase."

Let the record show that the "three-legged stool" of Benjamin Franklin and Thomas Bond in creating the nation's first hospital held the line.

Jon noted that while there would always be a vocal minority, it was rewarding to see that someone who was vocally loud against the organization, when you started talking the language of patient care, quality, collaboration, empathy, and compassion, the past kind of went away. That was rewarding. In Naples, we have endured this calamity in a community emerging from healthcare protest. As a leading healthcare organization, we became a major uniting force as Naples and Collier County blossomed into a tight-knit team of city and county governments, public and private hospitals, free clinics, physicians, volunteers, business owners, community leaders, first responders, and citizens eager to play a part in the battle against COVID-19.

Let the record show that the "three-legged stool" of Benjamin Franklin and Thomas Bond in creating the nation's first hospital held the line. Franklin knew that the only way we could be sure to put together an effective community hospital was to form a bond of partnership between the government, the organization, and the community, and keep it there. That bond was stronger in some communities than others and we believe Southwest Florida has been and will continue to be among the strongest in America.

Dr. Jim Mahon described the worst part of the pandemic for him: the daily feeling of uncertainty.

"I'm a long-distance runner and … I was always running anyway, but this became my therapy. I ran from 5:30 a.m. to 7:00 a.m. every morning for eight months. I needed to mentally and physically feel that I was OK before I came into the hospital."

The beautiful, long stretches of beach in Naples helped. Dr. Mahon thought of running as a "sort of physical booster shot" by getting in long runs on the beach.

"Because I'm now seventy, and I was worried just like everybody else. We all masked up. We assumed if anybody would get COVID-19, it would be us because we were in the hospital every day. But *knock on wood*, we came out of it OK."

Dr. Mahon describes that the NCH team avoided COVID-19 as incredibly lucky. It affects people differently.

"I've still got friends that have that COVID-19 fog. Or they still have bronchitis. It just gets any weak spot in your system and goes right to it and sticks to it. Including one's emotional state."

NCH general counsel Matt Heinle looked back.

"As we look back, and I have heard Paul Hiltz say this frequently, our board of trustees gave us a green light to do everything we needed to do, spend as much money as it needed to be spent to buy supplies, equipment, to compensate our employees who were most at risk when taking care of the sickest of the sick patients."

Despite state and federal financial help, it was still devastating to the bottom line.

"Our board never told us to hit the brakes in terms of doing what we needed to do, to do the right thing. It was extremely impressive, beyond impressive, because if you think about at the beginning of the pandemic, nobody had any idea how long this was going to last, how big it was going to be, how devastating to the bottom line for all healthcare systems," Matt observed.

The federal government led the way by having its finest hour in "Operation Warp Speed," which shaved years off the vaccine research and development and funded vaccines and distribution protocols and costs for everyone in America. The state government organized the vaccine distribution. The local government partnered with us on the *"All heroes wear masks"* campaign and the *"CommUNITY ImmUNITY"* campaign. Lee Health is a government hospital, and our inspiring partnership still pays dividends. Elected officials modeled mask-wearing and gave out free masks throughout the community.

On the "B side" of that heroic effort, the federal government also revealed its soft underbelly when in November 2021, the US Department of Labor's Occupational Safety & Health Administration issued a new 490-page document (repeat, 490 pages) to explain the federal government's new "COVID-19 Vaccination and Testing Emergency Temporary Standard."[83]

The community stepped up and joined together to fight COVID-19 by championing the heroes in our healthcare system, wearing masks and social distancing, and donating funds. The *Naples Daily News* and the local TV news teams became partners as we kept the citizens of Southwest Florida fully informed throughout the calamity. Donors stepped up and bought germ-zapping robots and vaccine freezers, providing vital funding. Organizations like Lee Health and NCH, which had yet to work together historically, joined into powerful coalitions to combat the pandemic.

Dr. David Lindner was credited, the newspaper reported in 2021, for his leadership in keeping the COVID-19 mortality rate low, at less than 150 deaths and more than 2,200 discharges, and only two employees were infected in the workplace.[84]

---

83   Federal Register, "COVID-19 Vaccination and Testing; Emergency Temporary Standard," accessed March 11, 2024, https://www.federalregister.gov/documents/2021/11/05/2021-23643/covid-19-vaccination-and-testing-emergency-temporary-standard.

84   Liz Freeman, "How Did NCH's COVID-19 Team Leader Win Physician of the Year? By Focusing on What's Best for Patients," *Naples Daily News*, March 5, 2021, accessed November 15, 2021, https://www.naplesnews.com/story/news/2021/03/05/covid-19-leader-nch-physician-year-dr-david-lindner-reflects-pandemic/4539159001/.

"I think we did a great job keeping our staff safe with PPE and protocols throughout the unfolding crisis," added Dr. Bryan Murphey.

New friendships were formed from mutual respect. Restaurants delivered thousands of free meals for the healthcare teams on duty. Doctors and nurses flooded the Neighborhood Clinic with volunteer service to ensure everyone in the community had full access to care. The community hospitals, as envisioned by Benjamin Franklin and Thomas Bond, served as the focal point for all this. We responded to every citizen in need. Hospitals fulfilled their role as the place of refuge, the place of trusted healers, as we were envisioned in 1751.

Dr. Peter T. Coleman, a professor of psychology at Columbia University who studies intractable conflict, observed that "during the Blitz, the fifty-six-day Nazi bombing campaign against Britain, Winston Churchill's cabinet was amazed and heartened to witness the ascendance of human goodness—altruism, compassion, and generosity of spirit and action." (His book, *The Way Out: How to Overcome Toxic Polarization*, was released in June 2021.)[85]

When we look back, we will see that some communities handled the crisis much better than others. We might well find that success came in states where government, civic and private-sector leaders joined their strengths together in a spirit of self-sacrifice for the common good.

—ARCHON FUNG, PROFESSOR OF CITIZENSHIP AND SELF-GOVERNMENT
JOHN F. KENNEDY SCHOOL OF GOVERNMENT, HARVARD UNIVERSITY[86]

85   David Kindy, "How Winston Churchill Endured the Blitz—and Taught the People of England to Do the Same," *Smithsonian* magazine, February 24, 2020, accessed November 15, 2021, https://www.smithsonianmag.com/history/how-winston-churchill-endured-blitzand-taught-people-england-do-same-180974229/.

86   Politico, "A New Civic Federalism," accessed March 11, 2024, https://www.politico.com/news/magazine/2020/03/19/coronavirus-effect-economy-life-society-analysis-covid-135579.

Can we predict the unexpected? Looking back at what we learned from the disruption and the pandemic, these two events have made significant impact. We cataloged dozens of our strategies and learning moments. Hopefully, by sharing these learnings with the community leadership in America, a different platform could emerge for responding to the next pandemic or the next internal disruption. In the very least, this narrative should change the conversation around branding and marketing in healthcare.

There have been many ways that COVID-19 changed the healthcare landscape entirely. We learned just how vulnerable America has become. All of us have a new appreciation for public health initiatives. To prepare our nation for the next pandemic, stockpiles of personal protection equipment is just the beginning.

From a brand trust perspective, we have a new appreciation for local physician expertise, backed by highly acclaimed experts at organizations like the Mayo Clinic. Despite having their finest hour on vaccine development, because of the polarization in America, there has been, regretfully, not enough universal trust for national figures, and the science backing up what they have been saying to us. As we look back, many legislators at all levels tried to make a difference, but got interrupted by courts, protests, and a polarized populace.

Wear a mask.

Don't wear a mask.

Mandates, no vaccine mandates: follow the bouncing ball.

In an era when political polarization conflicts with having national experts guiding the nation through a pandemic, the power of local expertise took on a new importance. There is a saying in American culture that "all politics are local."

Well, from our standpoint, all healthcare is local.

Perhaps many citizens prefer to listen to local clinical expertise because *this physician lives in my community* and has personal standing, a vested interest in exactly what we are going through. What matters most is not what is happening on the other coast or in giant cities, it's *what is happening right here.* Also, the local physicians share science. They do not shape their message to fit into a political motive, weaponize misinformation, or sensationalize.

NCH benefited from a fabulous team of clinical experts who made themselves available for media whenever needed. Even if citizens mistrusted the president, the governor, or national public health spokespersons, they universally trust our local physicians. In broadcast media, Dr. Doug Harrington, Dr. David Linder, Dr. Gregory Poland from Mayo, Dr. Carlos Quintero, and Dr. Paul Jones created a bond of absolute trust with a frightened community.

Because our culture, since 1918, has had no reason to fear indoor, confined human contact, it has taken the COVID-19 experience to develop a new appreciation for the effectiveness and necessity of tele-medicine. New broadband capabilities throughout our communities will eliminate some disparities. Access to computers for lower-income families is also on the list.

We have work to do with our hospital nurses, who have been gracious and loyal to their tasks, while traveling temporary nurses arrived by the dozen to fill in for vacant positions, earning a consider-able amount more per day than the full-time nurses. If the nation's acute care nurses are asked to continue to do this, facing a choice between a double shift or working beside someone who earns twice as much doing the same thing, sooner or later, there will have to be a reckoning.

⚒ PR TOOL KIT (AMANDA)
EVERGREEN COMMUNICATIONS

Communications can be a heavy burden during a pandemic. Our deployment of carefully developed joint campaigns with the City helped tackle tough problems like mask resistance and immunization. Everything takes on more importance when the message is sponsored by a partnership.

During the pandemic, we wished for an efficient way to capture physician commentary for television without bringing news crews into the hospitals. We created television studios to create our own content. We can begin to take our thought leadership, our clinical expertise, to a new level. Our instincts are to pioneer some new thinking on branding by having "always on," evergreen messaging where people can see it, learn from it, and be informed anytime, every day, whether in a pandemic or not, to help cultivate a healthier community. All this, on a device of their choosing. Evergreen content is a digital marketing term used to describe information that stays relevant over time. Like the trees, evergreen content is considered sustainable and lasting. On healthcare websites, examples of evergreen content could be how to lose weight, ten ways to help a baby stop crying, or how to tell the difference between a cold and the flu.

Bill Barker, the former president of the *Naples Daily News,* made a huge impact on the Naples region during his work in journalism here. After his departure from active journalism, we discussed the notion of community in the context of a healthcare provider.

What does *community* mean?

"We can shine a light on how this community has a deep desire to create a collective impact," Bill Barker noted.

"A great example is how over sixty of our largest businesses and organizations created community-wide impact on our children."

Bill's deep involvement in the creation of the Champions for Learning program evolved into the collective impact model that now has become known as Future Ready Collier, a network of more than sixty organizations, businesses, schools, and community members working to ensure every child in Collier County is ready for kindergarten, and every young person enters adulthood with a vision and plan to accomplish that vision. Every major institution, every major nonprofit, became deeply involved.

"It's all about getting all our arrows pointed in the same direction to maximize the impact of the work we do as a community."

"NCH is a major player in that. My point in that is that people that land in a position of responsibility over these institutions must have that community mindset for the communities to win. And I can tell you that most, if not all, of the people in our community that run our major businesses have that collective impact mentality, and they care about this community. And that's a big plus to Naples, Florida," Bill Barker said.

We brainstormed. What else can "community" depict? It can mean concierge. It can mean capable. It can mean capacity. It can mean being connected. It can mean commonality. It can mean a lot of things. It can imply trust. It can mean "local," implying that philanthropy will be applied to healthcare close to home. But it should not mean "small" and "unsophisticated."

And so, how do we take the word "community" and evolve it? We want to lean into this idea of being a community healthcare system, independently owned, nonprofit, with absolute world-class experts drawn to practice medicine here because we are among the most desirable places to live. We can make "community" look big, impressive, grand, noble, proud, and welcoming. It means we collaborate with our community, like Lee Health, the Health Network of Southwest Florida, and the Neighborhood Clinic, and each other.

🔧 BRANDING TOOL KIT (AMANDA)
THE POWER OF FOCUS GROUPS

The decision-making that revolves around rebranding an organization must be viewed from all points of the compass. While we adamantly recognize the power of the word "community," we also heard our top heart specialists telling us that the word "community" might interfere with the ability to attract top national clinical talent to Naples from Massachusetts General and Cleveland Clinic and Mayo and saying we're a community hospital would make us look small, and it might be a barrier to success. We heard from the community that they love our heritage and being a nonprofit community partner. It has not been that long ago that many withdrew their support when they began to sense that the leadership was not in touch with the community. This is too big a topic to make decisions without careful, organized input from key stakeholders. We commissioned focus groups throughout the end of 2021. We sought to know what the physicians were going to say, what the medical diplomats were going to say, what the internal stakeholders were going to say. We left our finger on the pulse.

Bill Barker's view is that NCH is on course.

He praised Paul's vision for the heart institute, the caliber of doctors he brought in to lead that, and where he is heading with women's health and orthopedics.

"All serve as great foundations for this type of community."

He observed that NCH has been creating a concierge referral business to bring all types of healthcare services here so that they're top-shelf all the way around. Also, Arthrex, one of the world's most impressive, world-class, sports orthopedic medical manufacturers, has worldwide headquarters here, another magnet for clinical excellence.

"No single hospital can provide 100 percent *best-of-case* care. They've got to pick and choose where they'll be experts, and I think NCH's focus on heart and stroke care is so important to a senior community like ours, where you don't have time on your side. Women's health and orthopedic advancements are also important."

Collier County's population is 33.6 percent over the age of sixty-five. Naples is 54.6 percent over sixty-five.[87]

General Counsel Matt Heinle looked back at the adventure of the previous two years, having joined NCH at the outset of the pandemic.

"I've never worked for a better CEO as I have with Paul. He has an extremely high level of emotional intelligence. He trusts his team. He's a wonderful communicator, and I love how he keeps the team small, too. It's a very nimble team, no egos, and so working for him and on the team is an honor."

Matt also noted that with all the consolidation in the healthcare industry over the years, "the fact that our board has said that we're going to remain an independent, locally governed healthcare system

---

87   US Census Bureau, Quick Facts, accessed March 14, 2024, https://www.census.gov/quickfacts/fact/table/colliercountyflorida,naplescityflorida/PST045222.

is fantastic, versus becoming part of some mega system that doesn't have any local governance or input."

He observed, "If you entered the pandemic financially weak, you are more than likely still financially weak."

Matt explained that NCH fortunately "has a solid balance sheet as we have wonderful donors. Our philanthropy arm of NCH is very strong. Our board has been a good financial steward of those assets. Being strong financially helps keep us independent, and we also have board leadership that wants us to *remain* independent."

The discipline of healthcare branding never stops, never pauses. It evolves. It responds to the organization's movement. It responds to the nation's sentiments. It responds to the physicians' instincts. We are looking closely and understanding that there may be damage from the pandemic there. Our nurses, our doctors, our technicians, and our first responders may have symptoms of posttraumatic stress disorder (PTSD). They have endured a major, life-changing traumatic event.

Many believe we have waited too long to mobilize for our warriors coming home from combat situations in Middle Eastern conflicts. For many, we assuredly have waited too long.

The burden borne by our physicians and nurses during COVID-19 is of deep concern. Highly respected CNN commentator Lt. Gen. (Ret.) Mark Hurtling delivered a keynote speech in early 2021 to a group of physicians weary from COVID-19 battles. Gen. Hurtling is the author of *Growing Physician Leaders: Empowering Doctors to Improve Our Healthcare.*[88]

88   Craig Gustafson, "Mark Hertling, SVP Lieutenant General, US Army (Ret.): A Voice at the Table—Training Physician Leaders," National Library of Medicine, August 2016, accessed March 4, 2024, https://www.ncbi.nlm.nih.gov/pmc/articles/PMC4991652/.

"This is a period where you're going to experience some things that you may or may not be ready for," he said. "These are the same issues soldiers face when redeploying from a combat zone."[89]

Lt. Gen Hurtling said that healthcare workers also have carried a load that has seemed unbearable.

"The things you have carried over the last year, plus as the pandemic has raged, will be with you in good, and sometimes bad, ways, and you need to address those things."

The *Naples Daily News* covered the topic of COVID-19 emotional damage in an article that appeared just before Thanksgiving 2021.[90] The article began with data from a Medscape survey of twelve thousand physicians, which found that 42 percent felt burned out.[91]

"Physician burnout is complex and costly, and it's unclear how much it will worsen in the uncharted territory of the pandemic or further erode quality of care, experts say," the newspaper reported.

Florida led the nation for many weeks in delta variant cases and hit a peak of 17,121 hospitalizations on August 23, 2021, according to the Florida Hospital Association.

Dr. David Lindner, medical director of the COVID-19 response team for NCH, fully expected some colleagues who worked in the COVID-19 units to experience PTSD, the *Naples Daily News*

---

89   Thomas R. Collins, "Military Leader Shows Hospitalists a Way Out of Pandemic 'Combat,'" May 4, 2021, accessed March 14, 2024, https://www.the-hospitalist.org/hospitalist/article/239588/leadership-training/military-leader-shows-hospitalists-way-out-pandemic.

90   Liz Freeman, "Is Your Doctor at Risk? Physicians Burning Out after Prolonged Fight on the COVID-19 Frontlines," *Naples Daily News*, November 17, 2021, accessed March 11, 2024, https://www.naplesnews.com/story/news/health/2021/11/17/doctor-burnout-covid-fuels-ptsd-suicides-poor-patient-care/6119468001/.

91   Leslie Kane, "'Death by 1000 cuts': Medscape National Physician Burnout & Suicide Report 2021," Medscape, January 22, 2021, accessed March 11, 2024, https://www.medscape.com/slideshow/2021-lifestyle-burnout-6013456?icd=login_success_gg_match_norm.

reported. While many businesses have put the pandemic behind them and tourism is flourishing in Florida, hospital workers have not moved on mentally. Caregivers and some community leaders seemed to be experiencing PTSD.

CHAPTER 8

BRAND BELONGING

In an era of seemingly endless possibilities for connecting with audiences, it's easy for companies to become overwhelmed and miss the mark on creating brand belonging.

We see it all the time: brands spread themselves thinly across every engagement platform, sharing seemingly disconnected content in the hopes of making any connection.

Should we be on every social media platform? Hop on every hashtag trend? Send out a weekly newsletter? Blog? Vlog?

A quick scan of social media content reveals what a brand is doing but gives no indication of who that brand is. Instead, it reads like that desperate friend who will like anything to be liked in return.

When your brand takes the try-anything approach, you do more damage than you think. Audiences can always tell when you're contributing to the constant barrage of meaningless noise instead of adding value. And ultimately, the customer experiences aren't creating a sense of belonging.

10,000; 8; and 21

We hold these three numbers up as a constant reminder of what we're dealing with in communication today.

The average consumer receives exposure to ten thousand brand messages per day.

Attention spans have dropped to eight seconds in the last fifteen years.

Audiences switch between screens up to twenty-one times per hour.

—The Partnership website
https://thepartnership.com/

With so much distraction, it takes more than a traditional brand connection to change habits and capture hearts; brand belonging begins when you give voice to your organization's value system.

That voice will become the most valuable communication you will create. It will guide your actions and instill purpose into everything you do.

When your value system becomes the foundation of your communication, you'll move beyond repeat customers. You will create true customer experiences leading to brand advocates. Stay consistent, and your customers will become brand champions who are real believers in who you are.

When value systems overlap, individuals experience a sense of belonging.

For instance, we practice what we preach.

Over the last several years, The Partnership has defined our values as Purpose, Passion, and Partnership. These values led to all our interactions with partners, employees, and even our company culture.

The defined values helped us to rethink our social strategy and relaunch how we communicate online. All this has caused a dramatic shift in our company and our work. It demonstrates values in action; it creates brand belonging.

So, how can you make brand belonging happen at your company? Start your journey with these important points:

- Define your value system. This isn't your list of values, mission, or vision. You build those things upon the foundation of "who you are."
- Know your believer group intimately, invite them in and arm them.
- Know your audience well, interact with them, and encourage them to support your brand.
- Create visible actions that support your value system and share.

Your actions should align with your values and clearly communicate these actions to your audience.

Purpose-built communication that creates belonging is the key to forging a strong and lasting connection with your audience.

By focusing on your value system and understanding your target audience, you can foster a sense of belonging. Your customers' experiences will go beyond mere transactions. Your brand will transform them into true believers.

The key is not to be present everywhere. Instead, focus on being in the right place with the right message that resonates with your audience's values. Moving from shallow involvement to strong connection will distinguish your brand, fostering customer loyalty and support.

Take the time to define your value system, get to know your believers and let your actions speak volumes. With the right approach, your brand can become a beacon of belonging in a crowded digital landscape.

THE UNIQUE APPROACH TO BRANDING BY NCH

This entire narrative is a fascinating case history, so it's quite fitting that we should conclude our story with the ongoing story of the rebranding of NCH.

It's not what you may think. We did not design a nifty new symbol and call it a day.

Our rebranding initiative began at an off-site board retreat in 2021. All our board members and the executive team were present. We listened to a third-party consulting company brief us on market trends, the forecast for our market share, where trends are heading in healthcare as regards outpatient care versus inpatient, and which service lines we can expect to grow over the years ahead. We discussed where we needed to invest and began building a new strategic plan for the organization.

There was discussion around the NCH brand and a very energetic conversation on why we might need to change how we identify ourselves. The discussion went on all day.

There were more informal discussions about this in the hallways, cafeteria, and at the water cooler. We were getting stopped in the hallways and pulled into brainstorming meetings about renaming, our logo, and our thematics. People wanted a say, but we insisted on a strategic process: market research. And more market research.

To supplement the strategic market research projects we had been using in human resources and philanthropy for years, the board approved research just on the name, and what the name sentiment and brand sentiment was related to the name.

So, in the summer of 2021, we hired an organization to do just that, and to present their findings to the board. Focus groups were convened both internally and externally.

So, we presented all this market research, and we went about all of this in a very strategic way, convening focus groups of stakeholders. We had a positive reaction to the brand, called a "positive brand affinity." We had more of a brand perception problem internally than externally. And so it really showed us that we needed to do more from an internal campaign marketing perspective, internal communications.

We certainly learned that coming out of COVID-19, we still have a lot of challenges. Our clinicians were fatigued. We suffered staff turnover and faced the downside of filling gaps with traveling nurses. This clearly showed up in our research.

We learned that our loyal donors had a huge positive affinity toward the word *community*, which was no shock.

We found that some of the physician stakeholders, subspecialists in particular, as well as surgeons and some newly arrived clinicians, wanted a big departure from the word *community*. They felt it would inhibit attracting the attention of the best doctors. They felt there were challenges in that they could not go to conferences and talk about where they work with pride because the word *community hospital* is very limiting.

Yet we had become something much greater: our array of new clinical trials, the research and advanced technology, the impressive outcomes, and all the innovation and advanced clinical medicine invested in this healthcare system.

We had been too occupied with battling the pandemic for the better part of two years to pause and reflect. Our language needs to get caught up with the nonstop advancement of NCH.

Months passed as we made sure that we had buy-in, we had engagement, and we had understanding and shared learning throughout the whole process. Our approach became a very strategic, thoughtful rebrand strategy process to make sure that we took the market research and the insights from that, and we brought everyone along in the process.

In 2022 and 2023 we started the creative exploration of coming up with the visual identity, a new brand look and feel. Our research demonstrated that we owned a positive heritage with the NCH identity, so we reidentified what it stood for, that it no longer stands for Naples Community Hospital, that it now stands for something that is much bigger and better and greater and bolder, and that is a comprehensive healthcare system.

So, NCH now stands for Naples Comprehensive Health.

Advanced Community Healthcare System

An organization that provides higher acuity care, has centers for excellence, conducts research including trials, provides graduate medical education, fellowships, has endowed chairs, and is focused on developing future physicians and clinicians.

So, we were able to keep the NCH. This turned out to be the most frugal alternative. Resources today are tight. And when you already have a huge market that is used to saying a certain name, or you already have such high visibility or market penetration, and you're not launching a new product or service … to get people to change what they call it is going to take a long time and involve a significant level of investment.

We earmarked zero net new dollars for the rebranding. The expenses were all baked into the current marketing budget. The stress and trauma of the pandemic has taken quite a toll on employee morale.

It would've been a heavy lift to try to get people to change what they call the healthcare system. The media, our donors, people inside and out, say "NCH," and changing that entirely was not advised. We all felt a need for rebranding. We had evolved.

Our medical staff has grown to over nine hundred physicians, and we now have medical facilities in dozens of Collier County and Southwest Florida locations.

The region is growing. The University of Florida's (UF) Bureau of Economic and Business Research projects Lee County to grow by nearly 24 percent and Collier County by 18 percent during the next quarter century.[92]

"Future growth in Southwest Florida will be due largely to record numbers of Baby Boomers retiring and migrating south," said an LSI Cos. analysis of the UF report this year. "Southwest Florida has and will continue to appeal greatly to affluent Baby Boomers looking for sun, beaches, boating, and championship golf," the *Naples Daily News* reported in October 2023.

Led by Robert Cubeddu, MD, formerly with the Cleveland Clinic, our heart institute is becoming world famous. Construction is well underway for a new $200 million heart center in downtown

---

92   Phil Fernandez, "Are Golfers behind Surprising SWFL Surge in Home Sales? And Who's Buying Country Clubs?" *Naples Daily News*, October 2, 2023, accessed December 10, 2023, https://www.naplesnews.com/story/money/2023/10/02/are-golfers-behind-surprising-sudden-surge-in-sw-florida-house-buying/70981273007/.

Naples, led by a gift of $20 million by the Richard M. Schulze Family Foundation.

In 2023, our plans met with a challenge created by local disagreement on the height of the building.

We are building a brand-new medical center for advanced orthopedic surgery with the New York-based Hospital for Special Surgery, ranked #1 in orthopedics for the past thirteen years by *U.S. News & World Report.*[93]

NCH is working in collaboration with Nicklaus Children's Health System, to upgrade the NICU from Level II to Level III.

We are also constructing a new inpatient rehabilitation hospital with Encompass Health.

Some of our nation's most distinguished physicians are moving to Naples to adjust their careers to a better quality of life.

---

93   HHS, "HSS Achieves Record 14th Consecutive National No. 1 Ranking in Orthopedics by U.S. News & World Report," August 1, 2023, accessed December 10, 2023, https://news.hss.edu/hss-achieves-record-14th-consecutive-national-no-1-ranking-in-orthopedics-by-us-news--world-report/.

NCH

NAPLES COMPREHENSIVE HEALTH

Mission

The NCH Mission is to help everyone
live a longer, happier, and healthier life.

Core Value

The NCH Core Value is to ensure excellence
in every patient experience.

We reported back what we heard in our focus groups and the findings of our studies. After many leaders' creative exploration and airing out dozens of symbols and logos, we ended up with something bold, differentiating, and visionary, articulating what we are becoming, not what we were.

The board approved a rebrand with the new logo. Part of that creation was revisiting our formal value propositions, how we state our values and vision, and really leaning into the mission. We made sure to define what that is, with all new messaging. We created a comprehensive "brand book," which sets graphic standards for using the new identity and providing that guidance and continuity to every manager in our organization.

We started "socializing" the new brand. That's the fun part where we show our excitement for the changes by telling stories, sharing the rationale and the new description of a community healthcare system. We told the story of how we came to this, making sure that everyone knew we are still there for the community, we're built by the community, we belong to this community, but we're not just a community hospital anymore. We're so much more than that.

And then we trademarked our term *an Advanced Community Healthcare System*™.

Our energy has been internal, making sure our team gets the whole story and can feel that sense of belonging. We are doing an inside-out approach. So, we first shared everything internally: doctors, nurses and clinicians, employees, board members, donors, community, and business leaders. Our biggest ambassadors are the people who work at NCH. We want them to believe in where they work, who they work for, and the product they're producing. It needs to be a point of pride in the quality of our healthcare.

We held Employee Appreciation Days, where we first shared the new logo and philosophy. Then we began to change to the new graphics organically, where there was low or no cost to change such materials as name badges, door mats, and digital information.

In spring 2024, we launched our formal (external) announcement on the new identity package.

So NCH approached this with patience and a new perspective. It's a textbook case on approaching the process in an economically conservative, reasonable way where you don't leave people out of the decision-making—Brand Belonging.

One of the best indicators is that we have had zero negative feedback long after its debut. Zero. We have honored the company's heritage and the organization's ownership by the citizens and have been frugal and thoughtful throughout. So again, we try to be as physically sustainable as possible, not by just burning all the stationery and business cards but by utilizing what we have in existence and then printing the new ones as needed, swapping things out as organically as possible.

NAPLES COMPREHENSIVE HEALTH

Advanced Community Healthcare System™

When we go to a philanthropy event or a donor appreciation social, these people are the plankholders. They have been involved for decades; they love hearing the redefinition of their community health-care system. The word *community* still has a big footprint.

It means something different to the physician world, where we focus on the advanced healthcare message.

Our conversation will always gravitate to the moments that matter when discussing employees. Those moments are decisions, dialogues, or events in an organization that impact the most on employee experience. We're on a heightened state of alert to watch for these opportunities.

We are alert to suggestions. When we encounter some pushback, we slow it down. An example of that alertness has been the slowdown thinking about new uniforms. During our employee surveys, we heard they didn't want to pay for a new logo embroidered on their uniforms. They also didn't want to pay for new uniforms if we changed colors. This dialogue created *moments that matter*. We pushed that decision to 2025 and assured the employees that NCH would cover all new uniform costs. We created an entire work group just around uniforms.

Despite over two years of battling the dark visitor in the trenches, our organization emerged with an enviable track record:

America's 100 Best Hospitals for 2024! This achievement puts NCH in the top 2 percent of hospitals nationwide for overall clinical performance and, along with being named one of America's Top 50 Hospitals for Surgical Care, reflects our commitment to exceptional patient care.

Other specialty awards received by NCH include being named one of Healthgrades' America's 100 Best Hospitals for:

- Cardiac Care™ for nine years in a row (2016–2024)
- Stroke Care™ for six years in a row (2019–2024)
- Pulmonary Care™ for five years in a row (2020–2024)
- Gastrointestinal Care™ for five years in a row (2020–2024)
- Gastrointestinal Surgery™ for four years in a row (2021–2024)
- Spine Surgery™ for two years in a row (2023–2024)
- Coronary Intervention™ in 2024

We also share the message that our *advanced community healthcare* is a great way to redefine what's possible and how that will enable us to remain an independent, nonprofit healthcare organization in a medical economy that challenges that value proposition every day.

This powerful narrative of an organization in crisis shows that the solutions lie with the community and the people on the front lines. If you rebrand the organization, you must listen to and make the case for support to every stakeholder.

Everyone.

PARTING WORDS AND FORECASTING SCENARIOS

CARLOS QUINTERO, MD

I am left disheartened because of the painful experiences of watching economically disadvantaged people suffer because of a lack of heart from their employers, a lack of knowledge, a lack of clinical attention, or a lack of trust.

While we spent every waking moment trying to regain the trust of a community and then proving our worth during the most significant healthcare challenge of the last hundred years, at the end of the day, I think of the migrant workers and poor people and how fearful they were of everything during this upheaval.

The hospitalist issue was more of a rollout. The intentions were all the right intentions. The problem was how the hospital executed the hospitalist unit experiment. They wanted to see if we could save the patients money and time in the hospital if they were under the care of a hospitalist rather than their trusted healer. The backlash came fast and hard.

Well-meaning citizens made signs and videos and wrote letters attacking the hospital leadership for abandoning their primary care doctors' right to see patients at NCH.

At the heart of it, an anti-hospital campaign was created to support community medicine. The fact that the community gathered protest energy when they felt their doctors were being treated poorly is noble and very American.

Recently, a colleague suggested that the very thing they were protesting ended up saving thousands of lives during the pandemic crisis: the team of hospitalists staffing NCH hospitals during our darkest hours, risking not only their own personal safety but also the safety of their families by serving on the front lines against COVID-19.

They were hospitalists. They had the training for this.

They endured, and for many, are still enduring the nightmares. Like the nightmare of a young mother losing her baby to COVID-19 and then later dying as well. The nightmare of realizing that if this gets much worse, we may have to decide who gets to live and who does not.

While a small army of community physician volunteers stood up and offered to help, that would have been awkward and complex, especially with dozens of physicians making patient rounds in our COVID-19 units.

The hospitalists got this.

Our already busy community physicians were responding to the non-inpatient needs of their patients, many of whom were scared to death of what was happening, especially older patients.

There's no doubt. And remember, hospitalists have been around for over twenty-five years.

I sometimes try to envision what the community's experience would have been like if there had been no hospitalists at all during the COVID-19 pandemic. Who's going to be taking care of these patients? Put bluntly, what would it have looked like if the vocal protesting citizens had resulted in the hospital eliminating hospitalists? Say they knocked it all the way out. Then, several months later, the deadliest pandemic in a hundred years attacks every single family in the region.

Well, if there were no hospitalists, there wouldn't have been as many advanced-trained physicians taking care of these patients in the hospital around the clock, and I believe that many more people would have died.

It's conjecture, but having been through what we have been through, this mental exercise leaves a scar.

I can't imagine us managing this crisis without dozens of our best hospitalist colleagues wading into this thing and caring for these highly contagious COVID-19 patients. I just can't imagine it. Yet, how close we came to being completely off balance when the day came!

So that's what we do. We, as hospitalists, take care of patients in the hospital. The many other internists and other physicians who normally don't see patients in the hospital had little time to give to inpatient care and management.

We did have an army of primary care doctors who stepped up to the plate and offered to come in to help, and that was comforting to see that we had that devoted doctors ready to come in if needed. And I know there was considerable relief that there would likely be no need for all hands on deck. Yet, at first, we had no idea. We had M.A.S.H.-like command tents standing by to increase hospital capacity. Everyone was on high alert for months. We had hundreds of respirators in storage.

Even better, the fact that we had a high-quality hospitalist program at NCH enabled us to hold back the community physicians in reserve until we were overwhelmed. The depth of clinical talent and excellence was there, ready, and quietly grateful that the chaos, while unrelenting, never overwhelmed.

AMANDA LUCEY

Your brand is your essence, your mission, vision, values, how you walk, talk, and what you deliver.

What an experience it has been to help reshape the NCH brand in a perfect storm of upheaval. The community sensed our excellence, experienced our sincerity, saw the heroism and self-sacrifice of our doctors and clinical staff, relied on our commitment, and felt comfort in belonging. It evolved organically and authentically.

COVID-19 will have the same societal impact as other cataclysmic events in America. We feel closer to each other, and we certainly feel that in Naples.

After the terrorist attacks on September 11, we changed many, many things: the way we get on an airplane, our surveillance of terrorist groups, our immigration policies, where we travel, the GPS and ID capabilities of our cell phones, which nations are our allies, what our military looks like, what our IDs look like, and what color the threat level is today. For healthcare, there has been an erosion of trust as the political divides have entered the healthcare space.

Much of that has been recovered because of the heroic job our healthcare team has done to face down the monster. Here is what matters for hospitals and health systems as we move forward: the vital development of the healthcare brand, our mission and vision, our values, our distinctive competency, and the earned trust of the people we serve.

Strategically, we will see a wave of new partnerships with community hospitals in America. The "stronger together" reality will replace the *perceived* aggressive, silent, competitive atmosphere of the past. We will still brand our services, advertise new capabilities, and make the community more involved in what we do. Still, the vital importance of the hospital as a focal point for the entire community in a crisis will change everything. The role of marketing and communications will advance to the highest level in leadership as decision-making and communications about that decision will be developed simultaneously.

Competition will remain but take on a new look and feel. All hospitals need to have beds occupied and a bustling emergency/trauma center. They all want and need doctors on staff who admit their patients to that provider. All this enables the provider to pay employees a healthy, competitive wage with robust benefits and keep up with advancing medical technology. Competitors will be on a playing field of quality and excellence.

Personally, I am a big Atlanta Braves fan. My Atlanta office overlooks the Truist Park field, and I could not help but feel a familiar feeling when the "all clear" was sounded following the COVID-19 crisis.

It felt like a 100 mph four-seam fastball-*high cheese* had just whistled past my head.

I knew this may not be the last time I would see that. And I knew we all had to step back in the box. But for now, we still celebrate the journey and the can-you-believe-it moments we all shared.

PAUL HILTZ

COVID-19 will have a lasting impact on our culture. I keep using the word dehumanizing. We don't get into conversations with people as much, which began during the worst part of COVID-19. Masks gave us a reason to stay to ourselves. There is still an element of fear present in our interactions with others. Rightfully so.

Prevention, which took a back seat in healthcare until March 11, 2020, will be heightened until the end of time. That will question who can work in a hospital or other provider environment. What does it take to be a healthcare worker? That answer may be changed. Now, people must consider whether to be in healthcare because it is dangerous. It has always been a career where solid training overcomes the risk.

In the short term (we hope), the supply chain and labor costs should level out. If not, those factors could threaten the very existence of many hospitals. In 2020, NCH received about $30 million in federal support for the pandemic. That helped. We will likely not see that again. Our demographics are very encouraging. Naples is a top destination for living and vacationing. We have fabulous physicians and nurses interested in moving here. This continues to be a very giving community in every way. The future is bright. There will be new sunshine on how we operate. Challenges once kept close to the vest will now be brought into the open air. Pluralistic management will share the authority to make decisions, ensuring critical physicians and community leaders are consulted at every opportunity.

On Tuesday, March 8, 2022, Lee Health and NCH hosted a joint press conference to commemorate the second anniversary of the coronavirus pandemic in Southwest Florida.[94]

We never ran out of supplies or beds and continuously educated our community, working with the City of Naples and other healthcare systems, including Lee Health. The *Stronger Together* campaign we developed with Lee Health demonstrated that we all pull together in a public health crisis.

At the ceremony, which was held at the Gulf Shores Medical Center, we all called for moments of silence to honor the 1,416 COVID-19 patients who've died in Lee Health facilities and the 377 coronavirus patients who have died in NCH facilities since the beginning of the pandemic.

The pandemic opened our eyes. To communication. To collaboration. To nurture community involvement. To listening.

Never forget Benjamin Franklin's notion of the three-legged stool to create a sustainable hospital. And never stop thanking our heroes, those who run toward the disaster.

And like Amanda says, we all need to step back in the box.

The *high heat* may return.

And I will step up to the plate with this team anywhere, any time.

---

94   John Davis, "Lee Health and NCH Systems Commemorate Two-Year Anniversary of COVID-19 Pandemic," WGCU, March 8, 2022, accessed May 14, 2022, https://news. wgcu.org/2022-03-08/lee-health-and-nch-healthcare-systems-commemorate-two-year-anniversary-of-covid-19-pandemic.

COMMUNICATIONS PLANNING

INTRODUCING PAUL HILTZ

Please help us welcome our new CEO Paul C. Hiltz to the NCH Healthcare System.

There will be multiple opportunities for internal NCH employees to meet our new CEO starting Thursday, August 1st until Friday, August 2nd.

Thursday, August 1st

Baker Hospital, Telford Building Auditorium
318 7th St N, Naples, FL 34102

10:00am – Meet and Greet Reception

3:00pm – Meet and Greet Reception

Friday, August 2nd

10:00am – Meet and Greet Reception
(North Naples Hospital, Board Room)

12:00pm – Meet and Greet Reception
(Central Campus Hospital,
Central Campus Conference Room)

3:00pm – Meet and Greet Reception
(North Naples Hospital, Board Room)

ALL HEROES WEAR MASKS

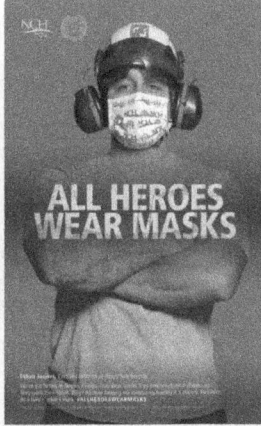

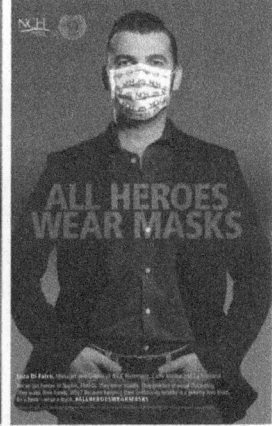

BE A HERO. WEAR A MASK.

It doesn't take much to be a hero. No, you don't have to fly, have superhuman strength or X-ray vision. In fact, anyone can be a hero in our community simply by wearing a mask. Afterall, being a hero means that you make the safety and well-being of others a priority.

That is why the City of Naples and NCH Healthcare System are counting on you to be a hero. Through our join initiative, we are inspiring our community to help keep our neighbors healthy and safe by wearing a mask. Because in Naples, all heroes wear masks.

Heroes also practice safe physical distancing and practice proper hygiene like washing their hands multiple times a day to help stop the spread of COVID 19. If you'd like more information on how you can help stop the spread of the virus, visit nchmd.org for details.

LEARN MORE

LOOKING FOR HEROES

Follow NCH and City of Naples on social and show us how you and your family are heroes in your community by wearing your masks.

Be sure to post your photos using #ALLHEROESWEARMASKS

NCH
ALL HEROES
WEAR MASKS
Keep our community safe.
Be a hero. Wear a mask.

NCH
ALL HEROES
WEAR MASKS
Keep our community safe.
Be a hero. Wear a mask.

NCH
Healthcare
System
ALL HEROES
WEAR MASKS
Keep our community safe.
Be a hero. Wear a mask.
#ALLHEROESWEARMASKS

NCH
Healthcare
System
ALL
HEROES
WEAR
MASKS
Keep our community safe.
Be a hero. Wear a mask.
#ALLHEROESWEARMASKS

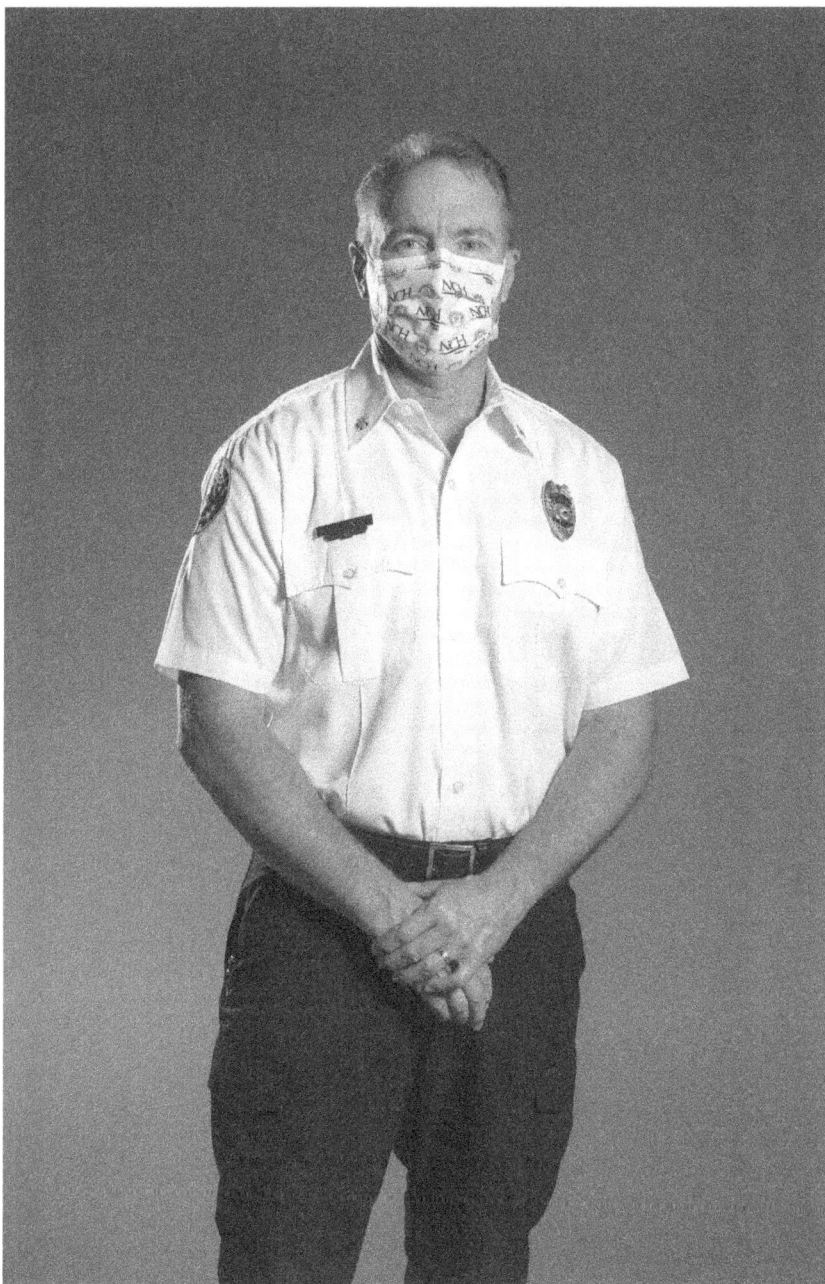

COMMUNITY IMMUNITY

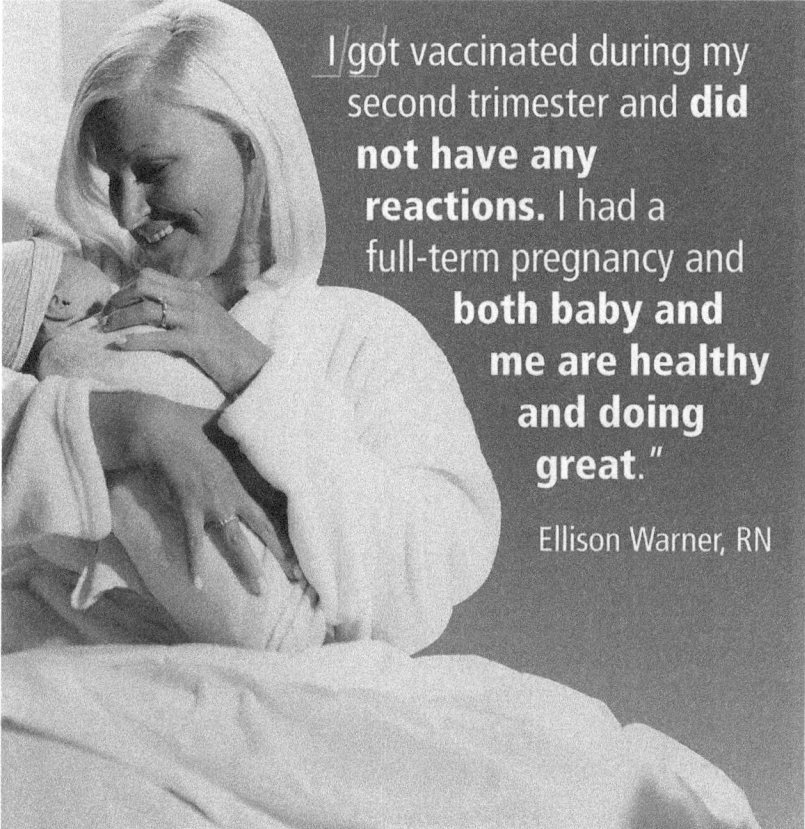

"I got vaccinated during my second trimester and **did not have any reactions.** I had a full-term pregnancy and **both baby and me are healthy and doing great.**"

Ellison Warner, RN

HEART

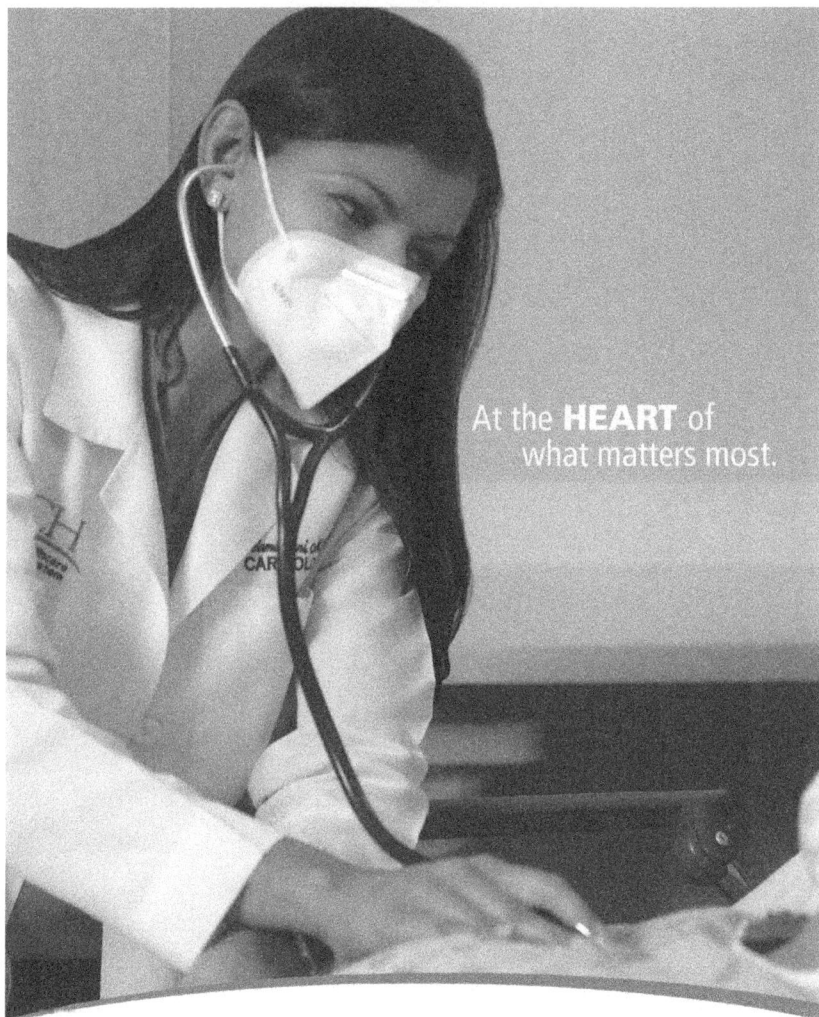

At the **HEART** of
what matters most.

The Difference Is In the Care.
At NCH Heart Institute, compassionate care is at
the heart of what matters most. From diagnosis to
recovery, our renowned physicians and nurses provide
a comprehensive cardiac care experience that is
unparalleled and had led NCH to be named as one of
America's 100 best hospitals for cardiac care.

NCHheart.com

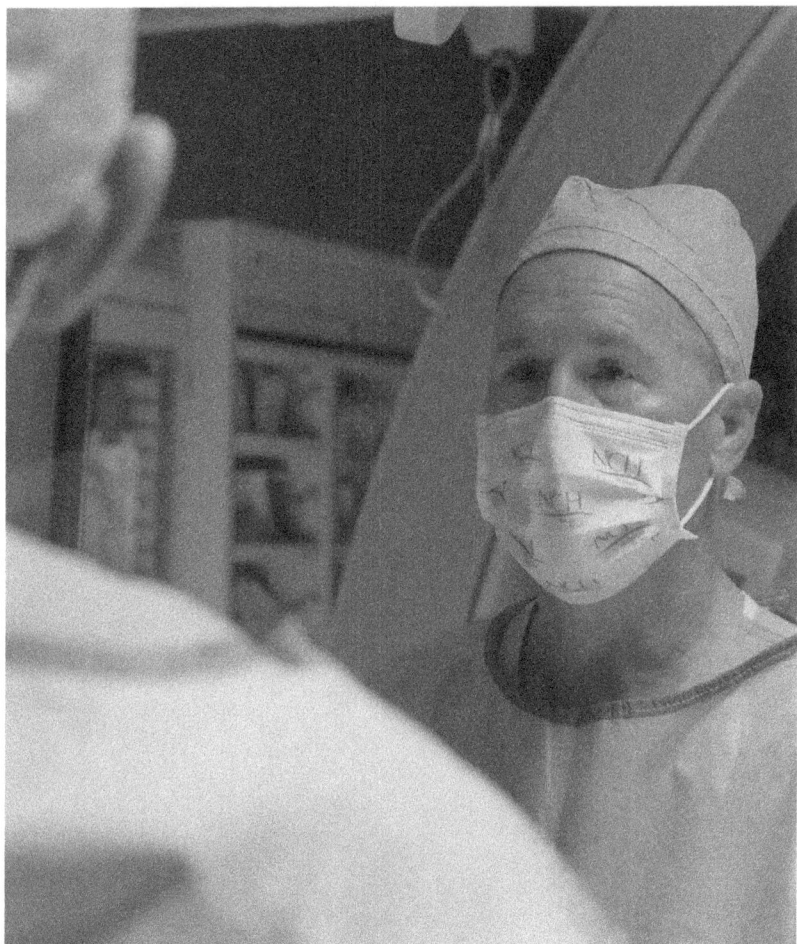

www.ingramcontent.com/pod-product-compliance
Lightning Source LLC
Chambersburg PA
CBHW031504180326
41458CB00044B/6695/J